W9-DDY-215

"In her brilliant new book, Margot Starbuck resurrects the concept of grace. She takes the face of God and shows us his laughter lines, she takes the hands of Jesus and shows us his scars, and she takes the heart of the church and shows it the kingdom of heaven. In short, Margot takes all the years of guilt inflicted by Christian legalism and replaces them with a message of acceptance, reminding each and every one of us of our true identity: beloved children of a heavenly Father. Following in the footsteps of the late Brennan Manning, Margot offers broken bread to a love-starved generation."

—**Emily T. Wierenga**, author of *Chasing Silhouettes* and *Mom in the Mirror*, www.emilywierenga.com

"Many modern Christians falsely portray God as a distant, disapproving, disappointed, disgruntled divinity. But Margot Starbuck pulls back the curtain on what God actually looks like. In *Not Who I Imagined*, she points out that behind the masks we've placed on God is a face of grace that accepts us *exactly as we are*. This book is a breath of fresh air in a world of stale spirituality, so if you're wondering whether to read it, I say, a thousand times, yes. It will help you put the 'good' back in 'good news.'"

—**Jonathan Merritt**, author of *Jesus Is Better Than You Imagined*

"Margot Starbuck's *Not Who I Imagined* is like a banner flying in the wind, championing grace and stirring the imaginations of the religious masses who often visualize God as a glorified sin auditor. Instead, Margot suggests God has a more gracious face than the one many assign to him. And the transformation he offers goes well beyond just a sin-cancelling transaction. The face of God presented here is one that is so wholly loving and deeply cherishing that it wipes away the chronic fear that lurks deep inside us—a fear that we are or will be found unacceptable. In faith circles, the phrase 'good news' is commonplace, but what *Not Who I Imagined* proclaims is far better news than most."

—**Sarah Cunningham**, author of *The Well-Balanced World Changer* and *Portable Faith*

"If you are a 'good Christian' who secretly worries that you aren't quite good enough for God's love, this book will confound you, delight you, and bring joy to your heart and soul."

—**Amy Julia Becker**, author of *A Good and Perfect Gift*

"Starbuck's imagination, insight, and truth-telling always capture me. She is a rare writer, one who empowers the reader with fresh, authentic insight."

—**Dr. Bruce McNicol**, president of Truefaced,
coauthor of the bestselling *The Cure*, *Bo's Cafe*,
The Ascent, and *Behind the Mask*

"In this lovely book, Margot Starbuck reminds us—with her brilliant wit and writing—of one of the most amazing aspects of our lovely God: that he has *a face*. A face that sees us, receives us, delights in us, and shines ever upon us, his beloved. A must-read for anyone who longs to see that amazing face of God all around us."

—**Caryn Rivadeneira**, author of *Known and Loved:
52 Devotions from the Psalms* and *Broke: What Financial
Desperation Revealed about God's Abundance*

"Fiercely bold and shockingly honest, *Not Who I Imagined* heralds the shame-shattering truth that the transcendent God who became visible in Jesus Christ furiously longs for intimacy with us: just as we are, right here, right now. For those longing to accept God's total and irrevocable acceptance, this achingly beautiful book will be like a breath of fresh air. I urge everyone not just to read it but to pray over it page by page as I have done."

—**Fil Anderson**, author of *Running on Empty*
and *Breaking the Rules*

SURPRISED BY A LOVING GOD

Not Who I Imagined

MARGOT STARBUCK

BakerBooks

a division of Baker Publishing Group
Grand Rapids, Michigan

Published by Baker Books
a division of Baker Publishing Group
P.O. Box 6287, Grand Rapids, MI 49516-6287
www.bakerbooks.com

Printed in the United States of America

Library of Congress Cataloging-in-Publication Data
Starbuck, Margot, 1969–
     Not who I imagined : surprised by a loving God / Margot Starbuck.
         pages   cm
     Includes bibliographical references and index.
     ISBN 978-0-8010-1494-9 (pbk. : alk. paper)
     1. Self-esteem—Religious aspects—Christianity. 2. God (Christianity)—
Love. 3. Shame—Religious aspects—Christianity. 4. Self-acceptance—Religious
aspects—Christianity. I. Title.
BV4598.24.S73 2014
248.4—dc23   2013034233

To protect the privacy of those who have shared their stories with the author, some details and names have been changed.

The author is represented by WordServe Literary Group.

14   15   16   17   18   19   20   7   6   5   4   3   2   1

*For my Doodlebug. May you always know,
in your deep places, that you are accepted,
received, and embraced—in each moment,
past, present, and future—by One whose
love does not, cannot, fail.*

Contents

The simplest of all remedies for shame is the discovery that we are, in spite of everything, accepted by the grace of someone we most need to accept us.

Lewis Smedes

Restore us, O God;
    let your face shine, that we may be saved.

Psalm 80:3

Preface

If I asked you to close your eyes and search for God's face, what would you see?

You might conjure the face of an NFL coach who just lost the Super Bowl: pressed lips, downturned eyes. This is the face of a god who lives with chronic low-grade disappointment in your subpar performance.

Or you might notice the countenance of the humorless, over-worked mom whose toddler has just poured pancake syrup all over the kitchen floor: flared nostrils, clenched jaw. This is the face of a deity who is frustrated by the messiness of your humanity.

But maybe the mug you see wouldn't be particularly accusing at all. Perhaps it would simply be distant, preoccupied with a smartphone or distracted by someone more compelling: eyes turned away, ears inattentive. This is the face of a god who is not particularly interested in you.

Maybe, though—just maybe—you would look into eyes that are altogether gracious. You would speak to ears that listen. In this face you would be seen, heard, and received exactly as you are. This is the face of the proud and satisfied coach. It's the unflappable mother who delights even in her child's mischief. It's the face of the beloved, turned toward you, that is reliably *with you* and *for you*.

Wouldn't that be the most wonderful face?

A lot of us have masked God with flimsy likenesses of the imperfect human faces we've known. Naturally, we need a little help peeling off the ill-fitting costumes we've unwittingly assigned to God. As we do, we at last come face-to-face with the gracious countenance, turned toward us in love, that *shines* upon us (Num. 6:25).

It is my prayer that this book can help you see and hear, with fresh eyes and ears, the face that is true.

Introduction

My Favorite Heresy

Best New Year's Eve party conversation starter ever: "What's your favorite heresy?"

I kid you not.

And while there were admittedly a few of us seminary-formed theo-geeks in the room, the fellow who tossed out this weird icebreaker was a normal guy. He was an engineer who, apparently, enjoyed noodling on theology.

My husband, Peter, and I were a little dumbstruck.

"Umm . . . " we each searched, wanting to come up with the most awesome, juicy heresy to titillate the room. We stuttered and stammered.

"One we actually *believe*," Peter asked to clarify, "or one we like to make fun of?"

"Either," the engineer granted.

Peter sort of babbled on a bit about scriptural authority—yawn—and when he was finished, none of us could identify anything heretical in what he'd blathered. It was sweet. He'd tried, but it had been a swing and a miss. Bless his little orthodox heart.

Sharon, our hostess, came into the room and asked what we were talking about. When we told her, she ribbed her husband, Anthony, and gladly offered, "Anthony doesn't believe in the resurrection of Jesus. Doesn't believe Jesus was divine. Doesn't believe in the virgin birth. Just thinks Jesus was a good guy."

Anthony, raised Catholic, was now an elder in his local mainline church. While I expected him to curl into a fetal ball of shame at being exposed, his proud grin communicated that he was entirely unflapped by it.

Though I wanted to hide my horror, and knew it was the socially appropriate thing to do, I was entirely befuddled by the news. I'd known Anthony for twelve years and, if you can believe it, this had never come up.

Unfiltered, I simply spit out, "No wonder the Catholics kicked you out!"

I'm not good in social situations.

Then it was the engineer's turn. As I'd hoped, his heresy was awesome. He believed the story of humanity's "fall from grace" told in Genesis was actually the story of *evolution*. To explain, he began by citing that, following the whole fruit-eating incident, the woman was cursed with an increase of pain in childbearing.

"Wait, wait." I stopped him. "You're saying that childbirth is *not* difficult for animals?"

I've watched *Animal Planet*. And all I have to say is: horse birth.

"No, the curse was an *increase* in the pain of childbearing. With evolution, the frontal cortex became larger. And in order to walk upright, the pelvic cage became smaller."

I was beginning to understand what he was saying. And since my pelvic cage *had* squeezed out a very evolved human head, it made all the sense in the world.

He continued to explain that what had transpired when Eve ate from the tree is that she knew the difference between good and evil. This is also what separates us from the animals. So what we call "the fall," the engineer believed, wasn't so much a matter of downward mobility as upward mobility. Instead of becoming *less* like God, we became *more* like God. More evolved.

Isn't this the best heresy you've heard all week?

My Stab at Heresy

Though I knew I couldn't compete with that breathtaking theory, I was kind of excited for my turn to share. A few days earlier I'd mentioned some questions I was having about the nature of salvation to Peter, but I hadn't tested them out in front of a real audience yet.

"Well," I began sheepishly, "I guess I've just started to have some questions about the way atonement works."

I waited for the walls to crumble and the earth to crack open, but nothing happened.

For the benefit of the few untrained theologians in the group, I explained, "Anselm's substitutionary theory of atonement would say something like: a holy God, who can't tolerate sin, demands satisfaction. So Jesus's sacrificial death, on our behalf, satisfies God. Then, when we receive Jesus, God looks at us and sees Jesus's sacrifice. It's what saves us."

As soon as I spit it out, I felt like I needed to explain more.

"I guess I just have this feeling that there might be a fuller way of describing what God does in our lives that is more comprehensive and gracious and thorough and redemptive than some of us have imagined."

There. It was out. And I'd not been swallowed up by a ball of fire. To admit all this in the presence of a resurrection-denier and a Jesus-trusting evolutionist felt like a pretty safe space. However, if this year's party invites are given to the people who were the most dynamic and compelling party guests last year, I might be sitting home alone come December 31.

Why It Matters

The way in which we understand *how* it is that God saves, how it is that God makes us right, matters—deeply.

Yes, God's salvation means you've got a spot secured in heaven.

Yes, it means God helps you to stop doing the bad stuff you've been doing.

Yes, it means God helps you to start doing good stuff.

But what if there's even more to it?

I have this sneaking suspicion that we, like the Pharisees before us, have been tempted to *narrow* what God is about instead of receiving the fullness of what God offers, the kind of grace that *expands* God's kingdom in human hearts and in the world.

Is it possible, I've wondered, that the One who sets captives free, who liberates people from the weight of sin and guilt, also helps those of us who find ourselves crushed under the crippling weight of *shame*?

Could it be possible that Jesus's life and death and resurrection might deal even more thoroughly with the power of sin, death, and shame—in my life and in the world—than I've even dreamed possible?

A Fresh Possibility

Because I want you to dream with me, I'll let you in on how I got to this place, this cliff of wondering.

When I was a college student, Brennan Manning spoke at a chapel service I attended. The way Manning narrated the gospel seemed too good to be true. Oh, how I longed to see the face of Manning's God, who was so gracious he smiled upon ragamuffins *as we are* and not as we should be.

For years, I held the memory of this grace in my heart.

Then, ten years ago, when I was in the midst of death-dealing emotional suffering, my brother had the audacity to suggest to me that not only had Christ come to deliver us from our sins but he also came to heal us from shame. Though it was the very thing I most needed and longed for, I, of course, thought it sounded outrageous.

Has he lost all his orthodox marbles? I wondered. *Everyone knows that Jesus came to forgive our sins!*

I really thought he'd gone off the deep end.

But the seed planted by Manning's gracious gospel had been watered.

What if Jesus came to forgive our sins and *also* to liberate us from so much more? What if Jesus really wanted us to know, in our very deepest places, that we were entirely and irrevocably accepted as we are and not as we should be? Not *just* at the moment that we prayed the Sinner's Prayer and at the moment we breathe our last breath and are jettisoned off toward heaven, but in every single moment in between?

Because, really, that—refusing, daily, God's acceptance—is our heresy.

Many of us have only truly accepted God's grace as being redemptive in our lives during these calculable bookend moments. We've been willing to believe that in whatever we identify as the moment of our *salvation*, we were—*past tense*—accepted by God entirely. Whether we believe we were saved at the font or in the gutter or in the pages of Scripture, we've been willing to agree that *in that moment* we were entirely accepted by God. Most of us who call ourselves Christians are also pretty quick to agree that, when we die, we will be warmly welcomed at those pearly gates. In the future we can't yet predict, God will receive us because of the sacrifice of Jesus.

> **What if Jesus really wanted us to know, in our very deepest places, that we were entirely and irrevocably accepted as we are and not as we should be?**

What about *today*, though? What about *this* moment?

The pervasive heresy no one's talking about is that, moment by moment, we refuse God's grace.

Though we'll concede that we *were* and *will be* accepted by the One whose acceptance we most need, we refuse to receive it *now*. We're quick to give it other names: we'll say we struggle to accept ourselves or we wrestle with body image or we have low self-esteem. We might even be willing to agree that this radical acceptance is available to others. Yet we walk around drenched in shame, feeling that we're not quite good enough as we are. And all the while, we already have been, and are, and will continue to be accepted by God exactly as we are!

Were we to receive this truth, were we to live, moment by moment, in the reality that God accepts us entirely—as we are and not as we should be—it would change *everything*.

What If God Is Different Than We Think?

Last year, at a friend's suggestion, I read Lewis Smedes's *Shame and Grace*. What spacious freedom to hear someone as reputable as Smedes dare to admit, "But guilt was not my problem as I felt it."[1]

I was not alone.

Smedes continues to identify the heart of his problem:

> What I felt most was a *glob of unworthiness* that I could not tie down to any concrete sins I was guilty of. What I needed more than pardon was a sense that God accepted me, owned me, held me, affirmed me, and would never let go of me even if he was not too much impressed with what he had on his hands.[2]

What? God might do *that*?

Sunlight beamed down on the little sprout of possibility that had begun to grow in my heart.

God's face, Smedes insists, is gracious.

In that moment, salvation through Jesus Christ became so much more to me than a sin-cancelling transaction to manage the nonstop unremarkable sinning I do.

I'd understood for years that God liberated dirty, rotten, no-good sinners—who'd murdered and slept around and extorted and bribed—but to hear that God gladly received mediocre sinners like me, who longed to be accepted, owned, held, and affirmed, was the gracious good news for which I'd been so desperately thirsting.

The sudden, fresh possibility of a God who sees me exactly as I am, and accepts me nonetheless, was exhilarating.

What if this was *exactly* what God was offering to me and to all who are suffocated by shame? What if, by locating God's gracious receiving only in the past and in the future, too many of us had missed the wonderful good news of grace altogether?

If God receives me as I am, then the good news is better than I had dared to imagine.

If, via the work of Jesus, God's eyes no longer saw me as being guilty, could it be possible that the same was true of my shame? Was it possible that the critical shaming eyes I'd internalized from others— ones that did not see me as

> In that moment, salvation through Jesus Christ became so much more to me than a sin-cancelling transaction to manage the nonstop unremarkable sinning I do.

worth loving—did not belong to Jesus's Father at all? *What if*, I began to wonder, *God sees me as entirely acceptable exactly the way I am?*

Smedes graciously discards the idea that God's eyes are like the pivoting lens of a hidden store camera, waiting to catch shoppers' sins.

"Suppose," ponders Smedes, "he is a watchful father who keeps his eyes on us, not to shame us but rather to save us and to be our friend. What then? Or," he continues, "is he more like a mother watching her toddler near a swimming pool and a father watching his daughter play the lead in *My Fair Lady*?"[3]

The possibility takes my breath away.

What if a gracious God is delivering us from sin *and* from so much more? What if Jesus's work on the cross—that liberates captives and frees prisoners—also sets each one of us free from shame to live into an abundant grace we've not yet begun to imagine?

It almost seems sinful, if not entirely heretical, to *not* consider the life-giving possibility.

Because if God is truly gracious, receiving sinners exactly as we are, we could, at last, stop trying to measure up.

And that would be fantastic.

Take some time to sit with this "What if" possibility. Make space in your heart to wonder, "God, are you more gracious than I have dared to imagine?" Open your prayerful imagination to receive what God has for you.

We're Formed by Early Faces

We long to see the face that is truly gracious, the one that accepts us exactly as we are, but our vision has been distorted. Because our worth has been reflected to us through human faces—critical, disappointed, distracted, angry, sad, or even absent faces—we may have perceived that we weren't worthy of unconditional love and acceptance. And we fail to see the face that is true.

1

The Face That Smiles

I f they want to see her, you'd better get them here."

The doctor's words to Holly's husband signaled that she had begun to die. Due to her Crohn's disease, Holly's paper-thin colon was unable to digest water. She'd not eaten for four months. Though exhausted, she'd been unable to sleep. She was tired and she hated what her illness had done to her husband and her two sons.

After her family left that evening, Holly decided she was ready to go. Though she was not a person of Christian faith, Holly did purposefully surrender and submit to what she would call "All That Is."

What Holly describes next sounds a bit like Hollywood's rendition of death, which they no doubt have gleaned from reports of real people like Holly. She describes ascending through the ceiling of her hospital room, through another floor, and then out into the glorious star-filled evening, caressed by the night air.

"Then," Holly explains, "I realized I was lying on something. . . . I put my hands down by my side to feel what it could be. I felt short hairs like on a knuckle. Then I felt what seemed like a finger, and when I felt what was on my other side, I touched another finger. It took a minute, but I finally realized I was resting in two hands—two very large hands that were holding me."[1]

What Holly quickly discerned is that those hands belonged to Jesus.

A Surprise Meeting

Holly is a friend of the family, and I can assure you that folks like Holly don't have encounters with Jesus. They chant and use Reiki. They visualize and master kinesiology. They throw around phrases like "positive energy" and "the harmony of all things." They do not encounter Jesus. Or if they do, they know better than to admit it in good company.

Holly explains, "I am not kidding . . . me, not religious, never been a big Jesus fan, wasn't even sure if I knew what he looked like except from old pictures on my grandmother's wall, but I was sure this was him. . . . The love was so vast and complete it saturated me with sensations for which I don't have the words to describe. The feelings were not of this world."[2]

Though most would call what Holly experienced "out of body," it was actually very corporeal. She touched hair and skin. She saw eyes of love. And though there was no audible voice, she claims that Jesus did "speak" to her. She explains, "He held me in his loving energy and let me bathe in it for as long as I wanted." Holly had, in her own words, "come home."[3]

After a while, Jesus asked Holly if she'd like to keep living her life on earth or leave with him. As she contemplated the decision, Holly felt as though she and Jesus were connected, with no separation. When she thought of her sons, ages four and eight, she knew her answer. She did not even have to voice it, because Christ knew the moment she knew. She explains, "Then Jesus gently covered my entire body with his breath, from my head to my toes, being very gentle and thorough. He then placed me back in my bed and left me snuggled sweetly and happily in my new world."[4]

Mmm . . . delicious.

A Different Face

Don, who'd been raised religious, saw the face of Jesus in quite a different light than Holly had.

In childhood, every time Don had erred, his grandmother assured him that God, who had a big book for this sort of thing, would put a black "X" next to his name. So it wasn't a wonderful "Book of Life" kind of book. It was more like . . . Santa's "Naughty List." Don admitted, "I know it sounds funny, but it was *scary*."

Despite the odds, today Don, forty years old, is a Christian. As if recorded in his deep places, even if against his will, Don's "God" now very much resembles his stern grandmother. When asked how he hears God and sees God, Don confessed, "When I hear the voice of God, the voice I hear is mean-sounding, very harsh. Like a really stern Puritan." The way Don *sees* God matches the voice, "In my mind I see God as 'Oz,' with all of that fire and thunder crashing around."

Until he married, Don kept these suspicions about God's character to himself. Not wanting to share them with people of faith, the ones so certain of God's goodness, and not wanting to share them with those without faith, for fear of ruining the reputation of the God who Christians insisted was *good*, he felt very much alone.

Don's pervasive sense of God's angry judgment had even affected how he read the Bible. He explained, "I have actually been scared to read the red lettering in the Bible when Jesus speaks. My English teachers graded everything in red pen, so there were always red, bleeding, scathing remarks."

Lots of people had English teachers. Not everyone had Don's grandmother.

He continued, "So, I guess because all of my mistakes were pointed out in red, it's like Jesus is yelling at me in red. In the words of Jesus I hear that condemning awful voice."

One evening, as Don was reading his Bible in bed, he confided to his wife how the voice of God sounded in his ears. Because he was a Christian, it felt almost shameful to say.

"I think Jesus sounds mean," he announced.

Confused, Don's wife, Janet, asked, "What do you mean?"

"Well, I was just reading the parable of the unmerciful servant," Don explained. "Jesus is teaching about forgiveness, and Peter wants to know how many times to forgive. You know how he asks Jesus if we're supposed to forgive seven times?"

Nodding, Janet followed along.

"But right here, in the red letters, Jesus says, 'I tell you, not seven times, but *seventy-seven times.*'" As the words passed Don's lips, they had a chilling tone.

Don confessed to his wife, "In my head, I hear it as a rebuke. Like, 'PETER! HOW STUPID ARE YOU!??! HOW UNFORGIVING ARE YOU!'" Tipping his eyes down, he admitted, "I hear it said with disgust and condemnation."

Don's wife gently tilted his face up toward hers.

Resting her hand on his face, she asked, "What if he said it like this . . . ?"

Calmly, addressing him with care and tenderness, Janet repeated the red-letter words, "I tell you, not seven times, but seventy-seven times.'" She really made it sound like good news. Tones of warmth and mercy resonated in her voice, as if she were assuring her groom, "You could screw up seventy-seven times—and seventy-seven *times* seventy-seven—and I would keep forgiving and forgiving and forgiving. I have a book with your name in it, lover. All that's written on each page is beloved, beloved, beloved. Mine, mine, mine."

When she stopped speaking, Don wept.

Too Common

When you tip your eyes to the face of God, do you see the face of Jesus that graciously welcomed Holly or the condemning one that haunted Don?

Without intending to, and even against our better judgment, so many of us have, like Don, given God the face and voice that once belonged to a formative person in our lives, masking God's true face with distorted shreds of faces we've known. We're *starving* to see the gracious face of love Holly encountered, but we've been unable, by force of will, to dismiss the stinging voice and condemning eyes nested in our deep places. Instead, silent and shamed, we give the lying voice and judging eyes free rent to live within us. And as long as we ignore this alien face, failing to look at it and question it and expose it, the false mask we've given to God remains.

Like Don, we've been reluctant to look into our own hearts to notice what type of God we've come to believe. If we're religious, the dissonance between what we publicly profess—namely, God's benevolence—and what we secretly hold in our hearts, God's judgment, can feel frightening. So we continue to tout the party line about God's goodness even as we fail to experience God's graciousness deep within ourselves.

Like Don, we've been slow to discuss our private wonderings about God in the company of other believers. To admit that we suspect God is mean or aloof or vindictive or abusive is to reveal what might be perceived as a weakness in our own faith. So we keep our hunches, doubts, and suspicions bottled up inside, giving them no access to air and light that could heal them.

> We continue to tout the party line about God's goodness even as we fail to experience God's graciousness deep within ourselves.

Like Don, to dare admit our ambivalence to *non-Christians* may feel like we are admitting we've concocted a deity in our own image. To acknowledge we've granted God the characteristics of various people in our lives hints that, where no God exists, we've shaped God out of thin air. To confess it feels like we're agreeing that we've made up all this "God" business to satisfy a deep primal wish for the daddy no one really has.

And even some of us who are able to see *Jesus* as gracious cannot fathom that his Father is, as we've been told, of exactly the same essence. Sure, they're *family*, we'll concede, but in sort of a "good cop/bad cop" kind of way. We don't *really* believe that the Father is as gracious as the sacrificial, sinner-loving Son.

And to admit any of this—to God, to ourselves, to believers, or to doubters—feels a bit scandalous.

Have you struggled to see the face of a God who is gracious? Has it ever felt like the God you worship bears an uncanny resemblance to the dad who left you, or the grandmother who shamed you, or the mom who drank too much? Feeling a very familiar sting that you never *quite* measure up, is it hard to believe you're accepted by *God* the way you are? Does the gracious God you sing about in Sunday morning worship songs bear any resemblance to the more insidious one lurking silently in your heart?

A Ridiculous Possibility

The first time I heard that a person's relationship with God might resemble a relationship with a physical human caregiver, I was about twenty years old. A well-meaning college classmate had mentioned to me that we naturally expect God to behave like our fathers had. To me the notion immediately sounded ridiculous. I was willing to admit that it was probably true for someone like Don, and that he probably needed to be delivered from it in some way, but I immediately filed such spiritual trivia away in the mental space marked "Old wives' tale/Does not apply to me."

According to the old wives' formula, I should have experienced God as one who'd abandoned me—but I didn't. Rather, at twenty, I was enamored with the person of Jesus and believed, with all of my heart, that his Father was good. What I did not realize at the time was that I had, for years, tacitly accepted *two* stories about my experience and about God. I was *aware* of one narrative while the other narrative was tucked away in secret.

The one I believed *consciously* was that by having so very *many* caregivers who loved me, I'd had the most *wonderful* childhood a girl could know. As the epitome of optimism, this is how it played in my mind. I had assigned the smiling face I saw in the mirror each morning to the face of God.

The more primal story, the one I'd internalized and kept hidden from others, was that I wasn't worth showing up for or sticking around for. It impacted my relationships with others and with God. Despite my dogged insistence otherwise, the countenance that I'd naturally assigned to God subconsciously was, after all, a composite sketch of the faces that had formed me—birthparents who'd relinquished me, a dad who left our home when I was six, a brother who left when I was twelve, a stepfather who left when I was sixteen. And the face I'd given to God, the one I refused to acknowledge, agreed with the human ones, both absent and present, that I wasn't really worth loving.

And though I once thought this human impulse to collapse the particular contours and expressions of human faces onto the divine One to be completely *odd*, today I cannot see how it could be otherwise. From the moment of our birth, we've sought a steadfast presence to receive us. It's how we're wired. We've longed for the assurance that God is *with* us and is *for* us. From the earliest faces who receive us, we've internalized what to expect from those who matter most to us. We've naturally assigned God a face like the ones that have formed us. Then, tragically, this masked deity has only confirmed our hunch that we're inherently unacceptable. Static, frozen, it has not been able to tell the truth because it has no life in it.

Like me, many of us continue to believe this lie about God's face until something or someone in our lives causes us—or allows us!—to recognize the mask, either the one we've been wearing to protect us from the truth of our experience or the one we'd given to God. Some of us have glimpsed the true face of God. Others of us came to recognize our own authentic faces. And, graciously, when one mask crumbled, the other did too.

This was, and continues to be, true in my experience. There's no formula for it. And, in fact, it's just like the chicken and egg riddle. For some, like me, the gracious face of God *that is real* is finally seen unmasked. Discovering in that moment that we are accepted exactly as we are allows us to lower our own cumbersome masks, which we've worn to be accepted.

Yet, for others, when we see the goodness in human faces we become able to recognize that same *goodness* in the face of God. As we encounter God's graciousness through human faces, and as God increases our prayerful imagination, we encounter his holiness and the masks we've worn—and the masks we've given to God at last dissolve.

The Possibility of Another Face

In these pages you are invited to consider whether God's face might look different from the one you've come to accept as real. As you read, begin to notice both the eyes and contours of the *face* you've assigned to the Holy One. Closing your eyes and quieting your heart, who do you see when you consider God? What do you hear when you consider God's voice? You are being invited into the possibility that God's face might be qualitatively different from any human face, naturally formed by sin and bound by shame, can be.

What if, unlike the other faces you've known, God's gracious eyes *actually do* accept you, warts and all, exactly as you are? What if God's voice affirms that, despite the lies you've swallowed, you are altogether beloved? What if, accepted entirely, you have absolutely nothing to fear?

That would be a pretty big deal, right?

About five years ago, my communicator friend Trina Pockett heard a conference speaker ask an audience to describe the expression they saw on the face of God. The responses he'd gotten were "God would be sad," or "He would look disappointed," or "He's angry with me." Trina told me that the feedback had surprised him—and it had surprised her too. Earlier in her life Trina herself had seen God with negative expressions, but over the course of time, with much prayer, journaling, spiritual growth, and good Christian counseling, her view of God's expression started to change.

Driving home, Trina reflected on the question that had been asked of the conference audience. *What expression does God have when he sees me?* When Trina got home, she found her daughter Kate in the bathroom combing her hair.

"Kate," she asked, "if God was looking at you right now, and you could see his face, what would his expression be?"

Without skipping a beat, Kate announced, "He'd be happy."

Surprised at her certainty, Trina queried, "How do you know that?"

"Mom," she replied, "he's *always* happy to see me."

Kate *gets* it.

And somehow, because of Kate, Trina gets more of it. And shares it.

"Margot," Trina gushed, "when I share this with audiences, there are tears in the room as people realize that they have placed a false 'expression' on the face of God."

> What if, unlike the other faces you've known, God's gracious eyes *actually do* accept you, warts and all, exactly as you are?

Beloved, my hope for you is that your eyes will be opened to the mask you've given to God. Poke it a little bit. Put a crack in it. Smash it like a piñata, if you like. Then consider the possibility that God's face may be more gracious than you've yet dared to imagine.

Close your eyes and allow yourself to search for God's face. The age, color, and contours are not as important as the expression you see turned toward you. What do you see? What do you hear? Have you seen this expression on another human face or heard a similar voice? Do this face and voice resemble what you know of Jesus's Father?

2

Forty-Two Bucks

When my boys were three and four years old, respectively, they were mesmerized by motor vehicles of all kinds. From the vantage point of their toddler-size car seats, they'd fixate on sports cars, pickup trucks, and motorcycles.

Spotting one zipping past us on the road, Rollie would stake a claim. "I'm *dat* one!"

Seeing another whiz past, Abhi would do the same. "I'm *dat* one!"

Identifying with stylish sports cars seemed to boost the boys' tiny little mojo, not entirely unlike two middle-aged men. Since I drove them around in a black Chevy Suburban that had large, groovy orange, yellow, and pink flowers on the side, I'm willing to concede that their mojo may have needed a little boost.

With increasing regularity, however, arguments would ensue.

"You not dat one! *I* dat one!" one would insist.

Within milliseconds the other would howl in righteous indignation, "*Mo-om!* He say I not dat one!"

Exhausted by the bickering, I eventually instituted a formal proprietary system: if the vehicle was blue, Rollie had first dibs. If it was yellow or red, Abhi could claim it.

Amazingly, this worked.

One afternoon, on the way to the store, we passed a local car dealership portside. I was the first one to notice a gorgeous, shiny, orange sports car, high and lifted up on an elevated platform. If I were a car person I could probably tell you what kind of a car it was, but all I can say with certainty is that it was shiny and orange.

As we stopped at a traffic light, I tapped my finger on the window of my door and whispered to Abhi, seated right behind me, "Doodlebug! Look!"

Noticing the car, he paused to calculate just what sort of resources he'd need to *actually* own it. I could sense that this was no longer a fantasy situation. He was really counting the requisite cost to park *that* vehicle in his own driveway.

By this time, my other two children had seen the dazzling sight.

Having noodled on it a bit, Abhi gave a deep sigh and announced, "If I had . . ."

He paused to do his little toddler calculations. Finally, he landed on a figure. I suspect it was the biggest number he knew.

"If I had . . . *forty-two dollahs* . . . I would buy dat car."

He said "forty-two dollars" like he could just as easily buy Jupiter with that amount.

But not really knowing if he'd nailed the price range, he turned his head toward his big brother to find out if he'd been close. Rollie, at four years old, just eight months Abhi's senior, was thoroughly disgusted by the estimate.

"It not forty-two dollah, Abhi," he smugly corrected.

The question, though, still remained. How much was the sports car worth? Realizing this, Rollie wagered a guess.

"It moh like . . ." He paused as he drummed up a plausible figure. Then, confidently, with dramatic flair, he announced, ". . . a *hundred* dollahs."

The figure was delivered as if it could have been a down payment on an entire galaxy.

Had the two boys been traveling alone in the back of the van, his pronouncement would have stood. But as the declaration escaped his lips, he realized that their big sister had been following the whole conversation. With four years of experience conditioning him to bow to her authority on all matters, he tipped his face toward six-year-old Zoe's big-kid booster seat.

Entirely comfortable in wielding her intellectual authority, Zoe replied with certainty, "More like . . . a *MILLION*."

● ● ● ● ●

We never *really* know what we are worth until we tip our eyes, and tilt our ears, toward the Face that is true.

● ● ● ● ●

As the words filled the expectant air, though, no one in the backseats, including Zoe, could be sure that she'd nailed it.

Six curious little eyes burned a hole in the back of my head, wondering about the value of the sports car.

It's what we do.

Not only do we tip our faces toward the next most knowledgeable expert on sports cars, we also look to other faces to find out what *we're* worth. We are wired to seek acceptance and understanding in human faces, whether or not they are equipped to reflect the truth to us, and they become the default repository of our value.

Some of these faces say we're worth forty-two bucks.

Some might even say a million.

And though, throughout our lives, we'll habitually turn to the faces of caregivers and siblings, teachers and peers, lovers and bosses to find ourselves in their faces, we never *really* know what we are worth until we tip our eyes, and tilt our ears, toward the Face that is true.

The Fascinating Truth about Pupils and What They Reveal

On one hand, it's metaphoric to say that we discover who we are in the eyes of another. It's the stuff of Disney fairy tales. But on the other hand, it's also true in a very literal, measurable way.

Since I'm already convinced that faces, especially the formative faces of our earliest caregivers, communicate *volumes* without ever uttering a word, I was curious to learn more about this. A few months ago, when I stumbled upon *The Definitive Book of Body Language*, I could not resist picking it up. The book described the science of pupillometry, which studies fluctuating pupil sizes in human beings. Eckhard Hess, from the University of Chicago, discovered that the size of the black circle at the center of the eye is affected by one's state of arousal. And while this ostensibly wouldn't change my life very much, its implications are actually fascinating.

For starters, our pupils get larger when we view something stimulating, whether a shiny orange sports car, an incredibly attractive individual, or an incredibly gooey piece of chocolate cake. And, it turns out, large dilated pupils are more attractive than tiny "beady" ones. Which actually does ring true of every illustrated cartoon lover, or beloved, I've ever seen portrayed in Disney films. Authors Allan and Barbara Pease explain, "The eyes are a key signal in courtship."[1] The benefit of eye makeup, then, is to emphasize "eye display." In the absence of beautiful large cartoon eyes, we make our own. But it goes beyond the makeup. "If a woman is attracted to a man," they explain, "she will dilate her pupils at him and he is likely to decode this signal correctly without knowing it."[2] (I told you this was good stuff.) It also explains why dimly lit places, like bars and restaurants—where pupils naturally widen—can set the stage for romance. Or sordid hookups. In fact, ancient prostitutes used eye drops to dilate their pupils to look more attractive![3] I'm not recommending this, but . . . genius!

The pupil dilation effect isn't just reserved for romantic encounters between couples. It's true of all sorts of relationships in our lives. We sort of "light up" at the sight of those things we find pleasing. For instance, when looking at photographs, men's eyes will dilate quickest to porn and women's will dilate quickest to images of mothers with babies. Go figure. That mothers' eyes respond readily to infants certainly *benefits* children. It signals to a child that he or she is desirable. Isn't that just the most marvelous design?

Pease and Pease explain, "Research also shows that pupil dilation has a reciprocal effect on the person who sees the dilated pupils."[4] This is important. It means that the pupils of someone staring into dilated eyes actually dilate to match the ones into which they're looking. We, very literally, *become* what we see in the eyes of another.

Our bodies, without consciously consulting our brains, are hard-wired not only to attract the attention of others but to *match*, to mirror, what we see on their faces. If we're on an eHarmony lunch date that is *not* a love connection, we perceive, in the eyes of another, that we are small. If the next online match finds us compelling, we know it because we can quite literally see it in his or her eyes. And as infants or children, like my own sweet ones in their car seats, we tip our faces toward those we trust and admire, and we discover who we are in the eyes of another.

A Theology of Mirror Neurons

This weird convergence of science and human attraction also inter-sect with theology. In a lecture delivered at St. Martin-in-the-Fields Church in London, theologian James Alison shares his excitement regarding recent scientific learning about mirror neurons, discov-ered at the University of Parma in 1996. He shares that Italian sci-entists noticed—via neural electrode wiring—that certain neurons in the brain fired when a monkey picked up a raisin.

Not to be a show-off, but I knew this *long* before 1996. I knew that neurons fired in my brain when I picked up a raisin, and that even *more* happy neurons fired if that raisin I picked up was covered in chocolate. Had someone baked those chocolaty raisins into a carrot cake, it would have been the Fourth of July in my brain.

The *surprising* discovery, Alison explains, is what happened next. While a monkey was still hooked up to electrodes, a scientist thoughtlessly picked up a raisin, as the monkeys had been doing. Perhaps he'd forgotten to bring in a healthy snack to work, I don't know. The scientists noticed that while the monkey was watching, the same brain neurons fired in the monkey as when he'd picked up the raisin himself. The neurons *mirrored* the activity of another in the brain of the watcher.

Not to be a know-it-all, especially right on the heels of already being a know-it-all about the sweet snacks, but there is also plenty of other empirical evidence to support this finding. If the research I've conducted in my own household is any indicator, this phenomenon is *also* true of children playing and watching video games. Often my offspring are as content to sit zombie-like beside a sibling playing a video game as they would be to play it themselves. And now I understand that it's because of these firing mirror neurons.

> We tip our faces toward those we trust and admire, and we discover who we are in the eyes of another.

Alison reports that research on humans now shows that these mirror neurons are fired off *from birth* in response to adult activity toward infants. He explains, "Within half an hour of birth a baby will stick its tongue out at an adult who sticks its tongue out at it."[5] Eventually, thank goodness, we'll all learn to moderate this innate urge. What's compelling, though, is how we're so fundamentally wired to download and imitate the behavior of others. And it's not as if we're watching an older sibling because we're trying desperately to figure out how to hit a fastball or do a flip off a diving board. No, we're recording all of this without any consciousness of doing so. What we're seeing is being programmed into our neural pathways.

To highlight that our imitation isn't just a kind of rote response that somehow circumvents memory, Alison cites another experiment with a baby who, plugged up with a pacifier, was temporarily unable to imitate an adult's expression. Later, when the pacifier was removed, the infant—who'd recorded the facial gesture in the circuits of memory—would imitate the expression!

This phenomenon, though, is so much more than a fun party trick, and the baby is doing more than merely thrusting out her tongue or lifting the corners of her mouth into a smile. Rather, the child is learning, *recording* in her memory, what she sees in the face of another. In the most primal way, it forms her. The circuits of this very deep primal memory record more than rote gestures. As she searches the faces of her caregivers, she is storing, in her core, the way she is or is not received by an *other*.

How We Are

As an infant, a child does not yet know herself to be *separate* from her caregiver. Unable to differentiate another face from her own being, the naturally egocentric child is discovering her *self*—namely, her value and her worthiness of attention, love, and nurture—from the faces around her. If the mother smiles and receives her, she's worth receiving. If the mother scowls and rejects her, she's worth rejecting. In the tiny infant brain, it really is as simple as that.

In this fundamental identification with a caregiver, an infant simply can't parse out what is true of herself from what is true of another. She can't discern that a teenage mother is overwhelmed. She is developmentally unable to understand a caregiver's clinical depression or a self-obsessed disinterest or an angry reaction to her crying and surmise, *Well, she's having a bad day*, or *Someone's about to start her cycle*, or *I wonder if there's any chance she could be borderline?* Instead, she swallows it whole. Sponge-like, the infant absorbs, entirely, who she is and what she is worth from the countenance of another. Alison ventures, "If an infant is perceived as a gift by its principal caregiver, then it will receive itself as a gift."[6] She will, quite literally, discover who she is in the face of another.

What Alison found so revolutionary about mirror neurons is that recent discoveries end the assumption that imitation is something we *learn* how to do. Rather, imitation of the faces around us is the *typical* way we discover who we are.

How We Are Formed

The reason I share Alison's excitement about these scientific findings in neurology is largely because these findings resonate with the thoughts of a thinker upon whom I already have a brain-crush. British psychiatrist Frank Lake suggested something very similar, decades ago, before all this excitement with mirror neurons. In 1966, Lake identified the ways face-to-face interaction with a mother *forms* an individual. Lake explains, "She creates in the baby, who innately desires this synthesis with the source-person, a satisfaction which gives the fundamental courage to be."[7] Through her face, the child discovers who he is.

This face of the mother, says Lake, is the face for which the infant naturally longs. Wired to imitate the most subtle gestures of her countenance, the infant's physical imitation is only a sign of much deeper layers of meaning that are inherent in the interaction. In infancy, the mother's face is the child's whole world. As the child grows, like my own car seat–trapped children, he will tip his face toward siblings and peers and teammates to find a reflection of his worth. Eventually, he will look to the face of a romantic interest to confirm his inherent acceptability. The child's natural human impulse is to mirror, to deeply internalize what he sees in the faces that matter most.

For better or for worse.

Who are some of the individuals—either present or absent—who reflected your worth to you as an infant? As a child? What types of expressions did you see on these faces? Anxiety? Acceptance? Distraction? Love? Anger? Grace? What did you learn about yourself from these faces?

3

The Making of a
Snack Closet Bandit

A number of years back, I'd traveled from my New Jersey home to Annapolis, Maryland, where I was received by college friends I was eager to see. Gretchen and Katherine had been among my very first friends at Westmont College. As Gretchen showed us around the beautiful home she shared with her husband, Katherine and I trailed behind her, Katherine tossing out silly-sweet compliments about Gretchen's lovely space. Along this tour, Gretchen signaled various rooms, with cozy beds, in which I'd be welcome to stay.

"Anyplace is fine," I chimed. "Couch is fine. Floor is fine. Wherever." My tone suggested that, had she thrown me down the stairs onto the floor of a dank, mildewy basement, I would have been quite satisfied and grateful.

Katherine got a little glimmer in her eye and remarked to Gretchen, "Look who doesn't want to be a burden!"

In that moment, my eyes opened to something I did not yet know about myself. In her harmless comment, I *saw* how I am. When traveling with friends, I'd jam my almost-six-foot-frame into the backseat of a compact car to give a much smaller friend the spacious front seat. I'd insist on sleeping on the floor, to free up a bed for someone else. When staying at the home of friends who were away, I used a ten-inch-square washcloth to towel myself dry after a shower, rather than use a fresh towel from their linen closet. If I ever *did* have the brazen gall to use a towel, I'd wake hours early the next day to wash towels and sheets, remaking the bed I'd so boldly accepted, so that there would be no trace of my existence. If I made myself unobtrusive and convenient and small, I would never be an unwelcome burden. Though I consciously prided myself on the fact that I wasn't one of these high-maintenance women—the kind who ride shotgun and sleep in beds and dry off with towels—the truth was that I didn't believe, in my deep places, that I was *worth* receiving.

A few years later, when I was reading Henri Nouwen's brilliant volume *The Inner Voice of Love*, the condition of my own heart, which Katherine knew long before I did, was revealed to me. "Not being welcome," Nouwen explains, "is your greatest fear. It connects with your birth fear, your fear of not being welcome in this life, and your death fear, your fear of not being welcome in the life after this. It is the deep-seated fear that it would have been better if you had not lived."[1]

I had navigated my way through a world where I was terrified of being rejected again by making myself small, my deep anxiety preventing me from ever receiving the genuine welcome for which I so longed. Though some of us have a gracious way of receiving hospitality, provision, and nurture—those whom I expect know themselves, at some level, to be *worth* loving—others of us aren't at all convinced we deserve to be received.

Receivers

I have long suspected that I'm not the only one who has ever felt this way. And what I've heard from gracious folks who've read and commented on my memoir, *The Girl in the Orange Dress*—about being adopted into a family with alcoholism, domestic violence, and divorce, and later finding my birthparents and being rejected by my birthfather—is that I'm not alone. Sure, their stories don't match mine, turn for turn, but something about my journey—the *human* journey?—has rung true for them. As I listen to the stories of others, I've discovered that folks who grow up in fairly functional families and fabulously functional families *all* wonder whether or not we're worth loving.

That *not-quite-convinced-ness*, in any number of varying degrees, is called *shame*.

In the life stories that others have so graciously shared with me, I hear that we all live with shame.

Researcher Brene Brown, who has much more authority to report on what she's heard in others' stories than I do, agrees that it's true. *We all live with shame.* Shame insists that we're not good enough as we are. It hisses that we're not quite worthy of love.

In her book *The Gifts of Imperfection*, Brown explains,

> The greatest challenge for most of us is believing that we are worthy now, right this minute. Worthiness doesn't have prerequisites. So many of us have knowingly created/unknowingly allowed/been handed down a long list of worthiness prerequisites:
>
> - I'll be worthy when I lose twenty pounds.
> - I'll be worthy if I can get pregnant.
> - I'll be worthy if I can get/stay sober.
> - I'll be worthy if everyone thinks I'm a good parent.
> - I'll be worthy when I can make a living selling my art.
> - I'll be worthy if I can hold my marriage together.
> - I'll be worthy when I make partner.
> - I'll be worthy when my parents finally approve.
> - I'll be worthy if he calls me back and asks me out.
> - I'll be worthy when I can do it all and look like I'm not even trying.[2]

I immediately want to add to her list, doubling and tripling it with my own insecurities.

- I'll be worthy when my birthfather realizes how fantastic I am.
- I'll be worthy when summer comes and my hair's a little blonder.
- I'll be worthy when my feet heal up enough for me to run again, like the worthy people who are *runners*.
- I'll be worthy when my next business takes off and makes millions.

I'll be worthy at some indefinite time in the future that never quite seems to come. Brown emphasizes, "Worthy now. Not if. Not when. We are worthy of love and belonging *now*. Right this minute. As-is."[3]

Pretty radical—and wonderful—stuff.

It's really the stuff of . . . *grace*.

Refusal to Be Received

To be clear about my story, I had an adoptive mom who loved me fiercely. I had a protective older brother. I had an adoptive dad who loved me before and after he stopped drinking and got his personal act together, when I was fifteen. I had grandparents who convinced me that I hung the moon. When I met my birthmom, she was bananas about me. Like many, though, the wily story I'd believed in my deep places, that I wasn't worth loving, had a very particular . . . stickiness.

So although welcome had been, and would be, extended to me throughout my lifetime, I had developed elaborate inner mechanisms to keep myself from comfortably receiving these gifts. When I would be suffering, with pain or loneliness, I'd always have an excuse why someone who might want to care for me couldn't or wouldn't or shouldn't receive me.

If I'd consider sharing my troubles with someone who seemed happy and satisfied with her own life, I'd thwart my own good intention. *She's so happy, she'd never understand my pain.*

If I'd toy with opening my heart to someone whose life was also challenging, I'd reason, *He's preoccupied with his own mess. He won't have time for my problems.*

When it seemed as though my therapist genuinely saw and heard and received me, the naughty voice in my head would say, *That doesn't count! You're paying her to look empathetic. So that's no indication that you're actually worth receiving.*

Or when I considered sharing with a *friend* who worked as a counselor, the voice chided, *Sure, he'll appear interested, but that's because he's a trained professional. He'll listen because he'll feel obliged to provide some "free counsel" as a friend, although he probably doesn't really care for you.*

When, at last overcoming my dogged resistance, there would be a living, breathing, caring person who *did* welcome me, listen to me, and receive my pain, I'd find a way to discount their real presence, protesting, *I know she's probably thinking about her job right now.*

He's been drinking, so his concern doesn't really count.

Even though she seems to be listening, I know she's more concerned with her own stuff than with my situation.

And after I had so vigorously denied the reality of the love available to me, the voices in my head would confirm, *Well, this is the way it is. You are left alone again. There is no one who is for you. You're not worth receiving.*

Clinging to an old story, I refused to release the one that had formed me. Despite all evidence to the contrary, I would convince myself it was so.

Seeing a Depriving Face

Ten-year-old Lucy (not her actual name), who'd been adopted from the foster care system when she was four, was convinced in her bones that she would never receive what she most needed. Each day Lucy would come home from school, drop into a chair at the kitchen table, and start doing her homework. One day, after school, she was chatting with her sister about walking a block to the store to get a bag of her favorite snack: Skittles. Lucy had tucked away in her Hello Kitty wallet seventy-two cents, enough money to buy a two-serving bag.

When Lucy's mother heard her contemplating the Skittles run, she quietly tiptoed upstairs. Unbeknownst to Lucy, she'd been to the store and bought a whole secret stash of Halloween fun-size Skittles for no other reason than to surprise and delight Lucy from time to time.

Lucy was still hammering away at long division when a little bag of Skittles, released from her mom's hands, fell from the sky and landed beside her math notebook.

Lucy took one look at the Skittles and threw herself facedown on the table. Full of despair, Lucy was unable to recognize the serving of rainbow candy that landed five inches from her hand as anything other than a sure sign that she never had, and never would, get what she wanted. Lucy's mother later discovered her daughter had been imagining a *big* two-serving bag from the corner store and her mom had offered her a *small* bag. Barraged by an old story, a voice hissed in Lucy's head, *See? You didn't get what you wanted. You're not seen, known, loved. You never will be, either.*

These voices can be really insidious.

Another child might have said, "Thanks, Mom."

Yet another might have said, "I really had my heart set on a big bag today. I'll wait and get some at the store."

And another one might have rejoiced. "Awesome! I've got seventy-two cents upstairs, so today I'm getting THREE servings!" (Picture ecstatic child doing some happy-dance.)

Not Lucy. Unable to recognize a gracious face, she saw only absence and want. For Lucy, the story she'd believed was a double-edged sword. She was unable to see someone who cared as a reliable provider, and she was unable to see herself as being worthy of good provision.

I tell you, it is a wily bind.

Faces during the Foundation Year

Like Lucy, via my own earliest face-to-face encounters where I did not recognize myself as being fully received, I had believed a nasty web of lies about myself. I believed that I wasn't worth receiving. No new evidence to the contrary would convince me.

One lie was about *me*: I wasn't worth loving. The other lie was about the person in my life who was, in that moment, my significant other. I believed that this person would not, or could not, love me. I simply had no tools to parse apart the sort of person I'd decided *I* was, the unworthy kind that people reject, from the people with whom I was in relationship.

Frank Lake maintains that these memories "of supposedly or actually unloving faces" from our earliest days are at the root of our unbelief, our defenses, and much of what becomes our sin.[4] My own formative memories during my first year, ones engraved in my deep places to which I did not even have conscious access, were at the root of what Lake would call my "compulsive unbelief." I now suspect that these faces—of the mother who gave me birth, and of shift nurses and a foster mother—were not, as Lake cedes, *actually* unloving, but in the wake of each absence, I *assumed* them to be.

The lie we believe, from faces both present and absent, is that we are not acceptable as we are. The faces to which we turn do not even have to fail us in very grand ways for our anxieties about not being received to be triggered. In fact, according to Lake, we need only "suppose" the faces to be unloving.

Things Change

For some of us, our deep longing to be received without reservation and without condition actually *is* met, for a time, by human faces. For a period, a lot of us look into a face that—no matter what we do—*delights* in who we are.

For a period, from the moment we open our little eyes in the morning, two big happy ones are locked on us. Sometimes four.

After bath time, as we're being clothed, a large mouth covers our face and belly with sloppy wet kisses. She delights in the rolls of fat around our thighs and wrists. The face feigns shock when we burp, but we can still tell that she is secretly pleased we've achieved such an impressive feat. And for a while, the face even lights up if we poop in our pants. Sort of like we've just completed a masterpiece to rival Michelangelo's Sistine Chapel ceiling.

Then things change.

And, to be fair, they have to.

One day the face that was once so pleased to see us every moment now looks sort of angry that we've woken up chipper and ready to start the day at 4:41 a.m. Again.

If we've attempted to dress ourselves the face may be disappointed when she assesses our combination of patterns or mismatched socks.

The one that loved our naked fat bodies now smacks the same chubby little hand that is reaching for a third cookie.

When we burp at the table, a brow furrows.

When we admit that we've soiled our pants, the face, once gracious, now looks angry.

Though a lot of us start out receiving exactly what we want and need, the faces to which we turn—human—are simply not equipped to extend unwavering unconditional love and acceptance. Nor, I am certain, should they be.

Frank Lake describes the deep longing of each heart: "that a true and loving maternal source accepts every aspect of the divided child's personality."[5] When we smile and play and serve and hug, we long to be accepted. When we do the things bodies are designed to do—wake and eliminate and get dressed and burp air—we long to be accepted. And even when we're naughty, we long to be accepted. Our divided selves—our loving, conniving, generous, willful, divided selves—long to be received by a gracious source that accepts every aspect of us.

It's important to note that even those of us with the most resourced caregivers experience a discrepancy between the kind of gracious unfailing reception for which we *long* and whatever it is we've *received*.

This isn't to whine or gripe. It's simply to acknowledge the inherent fallibility of human beings. Those of us who've received the best human nurture the world has to offer have not received unflagging unconditional welcome in every moment. A tired parent will rage. A Sunday school teacher will scold. A coach will shame. A sibling will despise. And because we're naturally wired with a sensitivity toward rejection, those fleeting moments have an unwieldy amount of *stick* to them!

> Our divided selves—our loving, conniving, generous, willful, divided selves—long to be received by a gracious source that accepts every aspect of us.

Other children, those with caregivers who lack adequate emotional resources—because they themselves were raised by caregivers who lacked emotional resources—do not receive anything close to what they most need. And yet these are the faces that will, necessarily, teach them whether or not they're worth receiving.

If a parent's eyes are glazed over while high on crack, a child concludes that he is not worth seeing.

If a parent's ears are constantly plugged with a Bluetooth phone, a child assumes that she is not worth hearing.

If a child's parent is absent to the office, he may naturally believe he's not worth showing up for.

If a child loses a parent to divorce or death, she may believe that she's not worth sticking around for.

If a parent gives herself over to her love of alcohol or shopping or extramarital relationships, a child may naturally believe that he's not worth loving.

For these children, the discrepancy between the kind, steadfast loving presence for which we yearn and what is actually received is pretty big.

Grocery Store Giving

Dr. James Loder, with whom I studied at Princeton Seminary, told our class, and *every* class, a story about an encounter he'd witnessed at the grocery store checkout line. Something about the veracity of this mundane story has stuck with me for twenty years.

An elderly person, tired, weary, face drawn, joins the checkout line behind a mother with a baby. The mother, busy with her groceries, is preoccupied. When the infant and the elderly man make eye contact, the man's entire countenance transforms. His face softens, his eyebrows raise, and his eyes widen. He begins cooing and making affectionate baby talk to the infant, who delights in the attention.

The infant's face had met the man's, and responded to the man, in a way in which most adult faces did not. More often, when adult faces make eye contact on the street, we glance briefly and then turn away. The baby, though, has not yet learned shyness. She's not yet learned to turn away. The infant is able to welcome the man fully, receiving him in a way that no other face in his life does. She holds his gaze and receives him. She represents the unfailing gaze for which we longed as infants, and which we later seek in a lover's eyes.

Don't you just want to go borrow someone's baby *right now*?

We long for the face that is fully prepared to receive us exactly as we are. That baby didn't care if the man worked as a custodian or a CEO. It didn't matter if he'd been cruel to his children or abundantly kind. The baby didn't care if he was going home to read the Bible or to drink himself into a stupor. The infant's completely accepting gaze is one that touches the deep places in our hearts.

Being Fully Received

When my eyes were opened in a hallway outside of Gretchen's guest room, in the wake of Katherine's sassy little remark, I finally saw

49

this unsavory thing about myself. I began to realize that I didn't *really* believe I was worth receiving. I'd internalized eyes that I supposed had communicated, *You're not really worth loving.* For years I had been low-maintenance, not by any virtue, but because I didn't believe I was worth caring for. After this eye-opening experience, and perhaps as a result of it, I've had a lot of healing happen in my life.

In fact, in the years since I first visited Gretchen, staying at her home has become somewhat of a barometer for me of the degree to which I've embraced the reality of being welcomed by another. When, at the core of my being, I did not know myself to be worthy of love, I behaved as if I was a burden. I'm pretty sure that on this occasion, and so many others, I'd been a real pain. But as God's own unconditional welcome has become real to me, I've come to know deep down inside that I'm worthy of being received by others.

A few years ago I invited myself to stay in the fabulous newly constructed mother-in-law suite in the basement of Gretchen's home. It's gorgeous. Throughout my stay I helped myself to drinks from the fridge, Halloween candy from the cabinet, and other treats from the snack closet. I tell you, I lived large in that suite.

As I dashed out to my car in the morning, Gretchen thoughtfully offered me breakfast and snacks for the road.

"Thanks, I already loaded up downstairs," I assured her, with sparkling soda water in hand and backpack stuffed with bags of animal cookies and cheesy crackers.

> As God's own unconditional welcome has become real to me, I've come to know deep down inside that I'm worthy of being received by others.

My eyes were once again opened, this time to a new reality. In this second, complementary, holy moment, I was able to see myself as I was—not through the eyes given to me by early others, but by a face, the one right in front of me, which reflected my inherent value.

Today I am so confident that I am worth receiving, *and* that my sweet friend wants to do it, that I live into the reality of my belovedness—and gain a pound or two whenever I'm at Gretchen's wonderful house.

Brene Brown writes, "The greatest challenge for most of us is believing that we are worthy now, right this minute."[6] How difficult or easy is it for you to believe that you are worthy **now**, right this minute? Do you carry "prerequisites" that you think you have to meet before you are worthy? What are they? Do you think God requires these? Pause to receive God's gracious acceptance for you in this moment!

We See Ourselves through Others' Eyes

Because we *do* come to know who we are through the eyes of others, we actually begin to see ourselves through their eyes. If the formative people in our lives were not well-resourced and able to receive us with unwavering acceptance—admittedly a tall order!—we may have trouble receiving ourselves as entirely acceptable and worthy of love.

4

Sophisticated Eye Transplants

Not long after we first moved to Durham, North Carolina, I received a pretty floral invitation in the mail. Ripping it open, I discovered I'd been invited to celebrate the birthday of a woman whom I hadn't known long. Though I'm typically not a big fan of parties, her genuine affection for me touched my heart. The surprise of being included in her celebration was a true blessing. But for some reason, I never called the hostess, a mutual acquaintance, to respond. I never wrote the date down on my calendar. The invitation simply sifted to the bottom of a pile of papers, forgotten.

On the day of the party, the first day of the month, I insightfully commented to my husband, "Can you believe we have a Saturday with *nothing* scheduled? I guess nobody thought to turn the page on their calendars to plan anything!"

I had no idea.

The next day I felt a pit in my stomach as the beautiful invitation came to mind. Furiously digging through the stack of bills and cards on the kitchen counter to find it, I was crushed to realize the party had taken place the previous day. I felt disappointed and ashamed. Though I'd been remembered and chosen, I hadn't *received* the welcome of my new friends. Instead, unable to see myself through their eyes, I'd weirdly re-created the old absence and rejection I still held in my bones.

The Rub

We discover whether we're worthy to be received from the early human faces we most trust. The way *they* see us becomes the way *we* see ourselves, and even the way *others* see us—even when it's not. The rub, of course, is that these formative faces are inherently inadequate. In critical moments—tired, distracted, sad, overwhelmed, angry, and fearful—they are simply ill-equipped to be the consistently gracious presence for which we long. As a result, we experience *shame*, believing we're unworthy of acceptance and belonging.

Honestly, it seems hardly fair that we're born with a longing for unfailing unconditional love and acceptance when the faces to whom we naturally turn are not able to meet the deep need of our hearts. Why would God, who is good, wire us this way, with this seemingly insatiable longing?

I've come to suspect we've been hardwired this way because our life actually *did* once depend upon being accepted by the gracious response of a life-giving other. To have been separated from them would have been terrifying. Brene Brown, in *I Thought It Was Just Me: Women Reclaiming Power and Courage in a Culture of Shame*, acknowledges the veracity of this primal terror. She writes, "We are wired for connection. It's in our biology. As infants, our need for connection is about survival. As we grow older, connection means thriving—emotionally, physically, spiritually and intellectually."[1] Physically unable to survive alone, without the warmth and food and shelter and care offered to us, we were wired, at the most instinctual level, to tip our faces toward those who could meet our needs.

We were wired to *survive*.

Everything about infant design lends itself to facilitate this early connection between the helpless and the helper. As babies, we had disproportionately large eyes to attract the gaze of a caregiver. The coloring of our features was more vibrant and rich than it would be in later life—shiny pink lips, dark thick lashes, rosy flushed cheeks—to arouse the eye. Our skin and hair, so delightfully smooth, were pleasing to the touch. Our compact noses allowed us to press right up against an offered breast. We were of a portable size to be conveniently scooped up and taken along. Should any of these fail, we were given lungs and voices to scream for out-of-reach attention. Completely vulnerable, dependent on the responsiveness of a caregiver, we were wired to attract and receive the acceptance of others.

> **Why would God, who is good, wire us this way, with this seemingly insatiable longing?**

Once, our lives actually depended on being accepted.

As we got older, that deep imprint—though no longer useful—remained. Well after our survival depended upon it, we continued to live with a low-grade, partially conscious anxiety about being rejected and abandoned by those we most needed to accept us. Hardwired to behave as if our survival depended on the gracious response of another, we continued to seek it. The absence of it felt, to some of us, like death.

Random, and Decidedly Un-random, Others

When patients narrate their lives to professional counselors, it's my understanding they often describe their relationships to other people. Though I can only speak with certainty about my own experience in the therapeutic space, this is how it goes. Even on the days that we talk about how furious we are at the woman who cut us off on I-40 or the surprising places our minds wander during church or a terrifying visit to the dentist, the assumption is that these feelings aren't *unrelated* to the people in our lives who are, or have been, closest to us. Those who are close to us, as well as those we randomly encounter, can all be considered as *objects* to whom we relate.

What was first noticed, or at least documented, by Sigmund Freud, was that some of these random "objects" whom patients described—the jerky bad driver in traffic, the old boyfriend about whom we accidentally fantasize during church, or a particular physician who evokes anxiety in us—were "loaded" with significance unique to each patient. Specifically, a passenger in my car on I-40, or someone else who knew the old boyfriend, or the hygienist who is scraping the plaque off my teeth, would experience each of these individuals differently than I did.

This isn't to say that we are seeing these people *clearly*. We're just seeing them differently. And psychologists would say that the reason we experience people differently has to do with an internal *something* that we bring to the relationship. That something, experts would say, is a prior relationship, or cluster of relationships, that we experienced long before getting behind the wheel, punching the time clock at work, or handing the overworked dental secretary our new insurance card. We are, the theory goes, unwittingly "transferring" something from the old relationship onto the new one. This explains why I missed out on a great birthday party. It means that our experience of other people is *always* determined, in small or large part, by what we do or do not bring to the encounter.

For me, this really explains so much.

It explains why, when I call tech assistance staff to help me troubleshoot irksome online website-building software, I can get sort of uncharacteristically furious at the faceless voice on the other end of the phone. And be so dead certain that they don't really care about helping me—and that the person's supervisor is probably *glad* they're not helping me—and maybe there's no one in the world who cares about me.

It explains why a series of visits to a string of doctors who weren't able to magically fix my health situation hissed to my deep places that these professionals did not care about me and just wanted my money and, probably, no one else cared for me because I wasn't worth seeing or hearing or knowing or loving.

It explains why, when I experienced a professional failure, I assumed that I'd be let go and that my supervisor would move on to someone who could get the job done and that this supervisor probably did not care about me at all anyway.

It explains why, on the "last" day of therapy—and, yes, in hindsight I realize that whatever I think will be the last time I ever have to darken those doors probably isn't the case at all—I assumed that my therapist would forget about me once I was off her schedule, since it was just her job and she most likely didn't care for me in the first place.

It's why, in the earliest months of my marriage, I half-expected my new groom to get hit by a bus. In my deep places I was expecting him to leave me, because I knew, with a fair degree of certainty, that I wasn't worth sticking around for.

Apparently, these thinkers are suggesting, there's something *I* am bringing to the table that keeps me from seeing someone else the way he or she actually is.

It's a possibility I'm now willing to entertain.

And, unfortunately, the idea that I'm somehow transferring something internal onto these "others" does sort of ring true. The scenario where I'm certain that the bad driver is only concerned with himself and doesn't care one whit about me, and that the fantasy boyfriend in my mind probably wouldn't care about me if he were real, and that all the uncaring doctors and dentists and therapists will forget about me the minute I leave the office, is how—regardless of reality—it plays out in my mind.

Theorists would agree that the unique template I'm bringing to each new relationship was somehow formed in relationship to important people in my early life. These early experiences that I naturally internalized give shape to my current relationships. Each of us are simultaneously living in two worlds, one external and one internal.

Unfortunately, none of these psychological geniuses are able to say, for sure, what sticks and why. Maybe it all sticks. Someplace.

My own experience seems to suggest that my early experiences that were difficult—and the stories I made up about those events—have gotten a wee bit more traction in my psyche than other pivotal moments that were filled with grace. It appears as though the expressions on the faces of important people who thought that I was entirely and altogether lovely have not had as much *stickiness* as the naughty whispers hissing that I'm not really worth loving. Those have been much easier to believe.

Regardless, the evidence gathered by researchers and the evidence gathered *every day of my life* has convinced me that the external world in which we relate to drivers and doctors, friends and family, are always impacted by our internal world and all the characters that populate it.

Telling Regressions

This kind of information would have been very useful to my husband during the early years of our marriage when I was prone to come atypically unglued. If we were watching TV and he'd disappear during a commercial to putter in the garage, he might return twenty minutes later to find a puddle of distraught soup where I'd previously been happily watching *Seinfeld*. Unable to move my arms or legs, unable to even call out toward the garage to inquire as to his whereabouts, I would regress to the state of a very young child, feeling utterly abandoned and forsaken. In my mind, he ceased to be the steadfast reliable guy I married and, in my deep places, became someone else altogether.

It appears as though the expressions on the faces of important people who thought that I was entirely and altogether lovely have not had as much *stickiness* as the naughty whispers hissing that I'm not really worth loving.

In *The Girl in the Orange Dress*, I share about the years preceding our marriage, which I had weathered wearing girl-size armor and a mask with a broad grinning smile. During the first six days of my life, which I spent in the hospital nursery with occasional visits with my birthmother, I was, as all infants are, uniquely wired to identify a single face that would provide reliable nutrition and comfort. In my circumstance, however, there was not just the *one* face of a new mom, but many faces—caregivers at the hospital.

After six days I was placed in a foster home. During those days I would have had no ability to comprehend "temporary care," so I would have quickly learned to recognize the face and voice of my foster mother as my primary caregiver. I likely bonded to her the way every other home-nestled baby does: recognizing her as a nose-snuggling, diaper-changing, bottle-feeding mommy. I would have begun to connect to my foster mother as my *own*. At three weeks of age, though, I was removed from that foster mom and given to another mom. And though every physical need was met, the emotional task of bonding to a single reliable adult other was . . . interrupted.

I don't know how long it took baby-Margot to know that this new mom was mine. For all I know, it was instantaneous. Had it been a movie on the *Lifetime* channel, I would have looked up at her, smiled sweetly, and the audience would have been able to breathe easy at the happy ending we all yearn to have. I have every reason, including photographic proof, to believe that I probably did perform the three-week equivalent of a sweet smile.

But we didn't live happily ever after. When this moment was *added* to the earlier ruptures, a part of me naturally deduced that I wasn't worth showing up for and I wasn't worth sticking around for. I came to believe that I wasn't *worth* loving.

The way I'd paste old masks onto new living, breathing faces is not at all particular to me. Radio host Garrison Keillor describes the way in which he had internalized the voice of his mother so that, even in her absence, her voice continued to speak. He writes:

> For fear of what it might do to me, you never paid a compliment, and when other people did, you beat it away from me with a stick. "He certainly is looking nice and grown up." *He'd look a lot nicer*

if he did something about his skin. "That's wonderful that he got that job." *Yeah, well, we'll see how long it lasts.* You trained me so well I now perform this service for myself. I deflect every kind word directed to me, and my denials are much more extravagant than the praise. "Good speech." *Oh, it was way too long, I didn't know what I was talking about, I was just blathering on and on, I was glad when it was over.*[2]

Keillor's subsequent relationships have been impacted by the physical and verbal presence of his mother in childhood. He speaks to himself with the gaze and voice that is most familiar and entrenched—that of his mother.

The Playdate That Never Was

Although the term "playdate" had yet to come into common usage when I was in first grade, I had one.

Technically, no adult knew about it yet, since Ian and I had just whipped up the idea at school recess. I hoped that when I called Mrs. Johnson, the neighbor who cared for me after school, she would okay it. Though persuaded by my friend to take the risk, I wasn't sure she would.

I had never done anything so bold as to make my own social plans. Yet, at age six, the wonderful mystique around going to a new friend's house had overridden my common sense. Who knew what kinds of marvelous toys, vehicles, and climbing equipment might be there? I was dying to find out.

After a long day at school, Ian and I packed up our tote bags and headed toward his house. A dutiful sixth-grade crossing guard wearing a neon orange safety sash waved us across the street. As we ambled down Main Street, we moved along the sidewalk in a pattern not unlike drunken bumblebees. There were, after all, seed pods to pick up, leaf piles to kick, and the wonderful, though rare, fallen bird's egg at which to marvel.

No six-year-old is ever in a hurry.

We were just two blocks from school when Ian and I both spotted the distant forms of two older boys headed our way on the sidewalk. The very fact that they had already been home and were headed back in the direction of school signaled how long it had taken the two of us to traverse just two blocks. Ian recognized them as older bullies from his neighborhood. I guessed they were eight or nine years old. They seemed very big.

Keenly aware of elementary school social dynamics, Ian and I both quickly intuited the situation. He did not want to be teased for having a girlfriend. No matter that I was the cool, tree-climbing, messy-haired, skinned-knee breed of girl. And I didn't want to be harassed any more than he did.

"Pretend like you're not with me," he muttered under his breath.

"Okay," I agreed willingly.

The strategy made all the sense in the world. Of course I would play along with his plan, lingering behind until the boys had passed. I'd pretend to study the houses I already knew by heart.

I was in complete agreement that we needed to pretend like we were *not* together.

What my body did, though, was something else altogether.

As if severed from my head, my body darted right into the speeding traffic of Main Street.

I ran into the street screaming, my arms flailing in the air like a panicked Muppet. It was like the pin to some crazy emotional grenade had been accidentally pulled.

Even more disturbing than a small child running into life-threatening danger was the fact that even as it was happening, the impulsive choice made complete sense to me. I wasn't upset by what Ian had said. My insides were calm. In my head, the dramatic show of hysteria would simply prove to those third-grade thugs that we were clearly *not* together. Darting in front of speeding cars actually seemed like the most logical choice in the world.

Thankfully, traffic came to a screeching halt and I was not killed.

My gratitude to the quick-witted driver who spared my life quickly dissolved into humiliation when she pulled her car into a side street to chew me out. She recognized Ian and identified herself as his neighbor. This lady *really* let me have it. I felt embarrassed and confused. When she finished scolding me, she demanded my name and address. I had no idea what she would do with this information, but I knew it wouldn't be good.

When she was finished with me, I felt much more shaken than when I was darting into traffic. After she drove off, I was so scared of seeing her again that I didn't go to Ian's house.

Ever.

Today, decades later, I still wonder exactly what happened inside that little girl in that odd moment when something took possession of a relatively sane, if not fully developed, mind and body.

My parents were separated, my dad had moved away, and, on the outside, I appeared very well-adjusted. I'd responded to the loss of my dad by smiling, armoring up, and soldiering on.

I suspect, though, that my insides were undone. And in that weird moment—when Ian asked me to behave as if we were not together, as if we were "separate"—I gave him another face. I saw myself through the eyes of someone rejected, and my bottled-up feelings about being "separated" from my dad seemed to explode like firecrackers.

Though I suppose I won't ever know for sure, I suspect I'd simply made visible the scary crisis my insides were afraid to acknowledge.

Have you ever noticed that you have "reactions" to people that don't necessarily match the mood or intensity of the actual situation? Describe. Can you identify an earlier person in your life toward whom your feelings or reactions—especially your anger or fear or sadness—might have been quite appropriate? Prayerfully offer these observations to God.

5

Pay No Attention to the Tiny Shoulder Devil

I'd been entrusted by my husband with the job of driving to the video rental store to select a movie. I take these sorts of missions pretty seriously. Pawing through rack after rack in search of some happy medium between a sappy chick flick and a blow-stuff-up action feature, I wasn't having any luck. I know I can't be alone in having difficulty with this type of assignment.

"There's only one left," I heard someone casually remark, one aisle over.

My heart rate quickened. *Only one left? Oh my gosh, how can I get it?*

I didn't even know what it was.

I eavesdropped long enough to deduce that there was only one copy left of a Bruce Willis movie from Disney called *The Kid*. Thinking I might get blow-stuff-up credit if I brought home a movie starring Bruce Willis, I sidled around the corner and snatched up the single remaining copy of *The Kid*. Even as I was doing it, I was a little surprised at myself. Neither my husband nor I generally wanted to watch a Disney movie, and neither did Bruce Willis particularly appeal.

Still, it was the *last* one!

Greed pushing me over the edge of indecision, I snatched it up and took it home.

The Kid

The Kid tells the story of the strange reunion of thirty-nine-year-old Russ Duritz, played by Bruce Willis, and his seven-year-old self.[1] Duritz works in Los Angeles as an image consultant, a Hollywood spin doctor who is paid big bucks to get public figures out of the messes into which they get themselves. He is arrogant, rude, and deceptive.

The young, innocent Rusty, though, is a charming, chubby little boy who has mysteriously stumbled into Russ's fast-track life. Russ—who identifies himself as a "high-powered affluent chick magnet"—labels his young self "a pathetic loser." The premise is that there is something between them that must be resolved before they can return, in time and space, to their proper lives.

> The face that lies comes to us in a myriad of subtle, and not so subtle, ways.

In the process, young Rusty, who dreams of growing up to fly planes and drive a truck with a dog in the back, tries to understand what the adult version of *himself* actually does. After spending time with the powerful and manipulative Russ, he ventures, "You help people lie about who they really are so they can pretend to be somebody else, right?" Right.

As the day of Rusty and Russ's eighth and fortieth birthday approaches, they attempt to discover the purpose of their odd reunion so that each can return to a normal life. When the day arrives, the two are thrown back in time to Rusty's childhood in the early sixties to revisit the critical moment that seems to seek resolution. What the adult Russ witnesses is his father coming home from work in an angry rage, shaking young Rusty and yelling at him.

Inadvertently this distraught father reveals that Rusty's mother is dying and blames Rusty for troubling her further.

The lie Rusty had swallowed as a child was that he was responsible for his mother's death. The face Rusty most trusted, undone with grief, had spoken a lie to Rusty's soul that had lodged deep and continued to fester. During his childhood, Rusty would bear two fundamental types of shame: he was shamed by a face that was physically *present* in his father's countenance, and he experienced shame from a face that was *absent* in the wake of his mother's death. From that moment on his life was dramatically altered by the enduring power of those two faces. Eventually Russ loses his true self under a web of posturing and deceptive appearances.

The Ultimate Spin Doctor

The face that lies comes to us in a myriad of subtle, and not so subtle, ways. It is the desperate language of a broken man on the verge of losing his wife. It's the fists of the cruel school bully on the playground. It is the face of the mother who longs with every fiber of her being to be present, whose broken body gives in to absence. It is every formative countenance into which a child gazes that whispers, "You're not really *worth* loving."

And like they did with young Rusty, the poisonous arrows fly deep into soft young flesh, landing in a child's deepest places. Untreated, they fester for years.

The face that lies is that countenance that persuades us we are other than who God has declared that we are. Whether it is a face that is physically present or one that is absent, it is the face that causes us to believe we are *less* than who God made us to be. A condemned sinner. Insignificant. "A pathetic loser." This countenance can also fool us into thinking we are godlike, better than others. "A high-powered chick magnet."

Like a Hollywood spin doctor, the enemy deceives people into masking up and lying—to themselves and to others—about who they really are.

Just as the face that lies takes different forms in our lives, so too it takes various forms in Scripture. In the garden, Eve comes face to face with a lying serpent. In the wilderness, Jesus has another showdown with the same character. Same guy, different face.

I have lots of suspicions about the other unnamed places this imposter was lurking throughout other pages of the Scriptures. I hear his voice disguised in those who insisted, "Gimmee a break! That know-it-all Jesus is *not* God's son."

I see glimpses of his countenance in the furious expressions of the Religious as they plotted against God's beloved. Every time someone said to Jesus, "You're not *really* who God says you are," the face that lies was present.

I am fairly certain he was lurking, pressing in on Jesus's garden prayer time with the Father, the night before his crucifixion. I suspect that as an uncreative sort, he used a script just like the one he used in the garden and the wilderness: "Are you really sure God's got your back? Probably not. There's another way, you know. Have you considered taking things into your own hands?"

The fourth chapter of Matthew's Gospel shares the story of Jesus's wilderness encounter with the deceiver. Much more difficult to recognize than Warner Brothers' horned red cartoon devil, the one Jesus faced in the wilderness comes to us today—as he did then—as a real smooth-talker. He's like the drug dealer on the corner or the crooked salesman who promises, "You can trust me. I've got your back. You don't need to experience one moment of worry or distress, because I can hook you up with real relief for your troubles. Once we make the exchange, it's all yours." These are the kind of lies that seem to make all the sense in the world!

Embedded in the enemy's three temptations is the lie that insists, "You're not *really* who God says you are."

> Taking advantage of his hunger, he says, "Since you are God's Son, speak the word that will turn these stones into loaves of bread" (Matt. 4:3 Message).

Taking him to the top of the temple in the Holy City, the tempter suggests, "Since you are God's Son, jump" (v. 5 Message).

And taking him to the peak of a high mountain, gesturing toward the earth's glorious kingdoms, he says, "They're yours—lock, stock, and barrel. Just go down on your knees and worship me, and they're yours" (v. 9 Message).

Please use the ears of your prayerful imagination to hear the tone with which the devil hissed, "Since you're God's Son." The implicit meaning, when these words drip off the lips of a liar, is the *opposite* of the words themselves! What's actually being said is, "You don't really think you're God's Son, do you? Are you sure he's got your back? Probably not."

Every single temptation is predicated on this premise: you are really *not* who God says you *are*.

The timing of Jesus's temptation is significant. On one hand, it happens when Jesus is—by outward appearances—physically *weak*. He's fasted for forty days. Members of Alcoholics Anonymous will confirm that we are most likely to give in to temptation when we're weak, hungry, tired, or stressed. On the other hand, though, Jesus's wilderness adventure happens just on the heels of his riverside baptism. When Jesus was baptized by John, the words that I believe had already been inscribed and nurtured in Jesus's deep places were, in that holy moment, made audible for the rest of us: "This is my Son, the Beloved, with whom I am well pleased" (Matt. 3:17).

That is the announcement of the face and voice that is true.

He belongs to me. He's my son. I am his and he is mine.

He is irrefutably beloved. I love this guy.

He pleases me. I'm satisfied with him.

They are the words, the reality, for which most of us are thirsting.

After this, Jesus had forty uninterrupted days to sit with the reality of his Father's unbridled affection for him. Though I believe that Jesus had been formed, prior to this announcement, the way we all are—by the faces of the earthly parents who reflected to him his belovedness, by the face of the Father he'd met in prayer, and even by men who'd reacted to him when they heard him teach in the temple at age twelve!—it was the spoken announcement from heaven that would be his only food, his soul food, for forty days and nights.

Jesus was very, very clear about who he was. That he was beloved by and acceptable to the Father was the most fundamental reality of his identity. His natural reply to the attack of the face that lies was to announce the true words of Scripture.

In Jesus's wilderness temptation, as it is when we're tempted to believe we're other than who God says we are, the voice from heaven whispers into one ear and the hiss of hell into the other. And as it is with us, Jesus had to *choose* whether he'd heed the voice of the devil or the descended dove reminding him of his Father's words. Jesus tipped his ear toward his Father, confirming, "I know who I *really* am: beloved. I belong to my Father."

Alternate Ending

The story that unfolds in *The Kid* climaxes on the day of Rusty's eighth birthday. He had heard the lying screech of the enemy from the face he most trusted, and what he most needed in that moment was to receive the truth about who he was.

Left alone outside, as his father storms into the house, young Rusty wanders back toward the older Russ. As their eyes meet, each realizes that the imminent loss of his mother is the critical event they were to revisit.

"Mom's dying," explains Rusty.

"Yeah, I know," confirms Russ.

"Soon?"

"Yeah, before your next birthday."

"Did I do it?" The frightened boy asks.

"No, no, you didn't do it. It's not your fault. Dad was just saying those things because he's scared. He knows he has to raise you alone and he doesn't know how to do it."

The lie that corrupted Rusty was "I am responsible for my mother's death." And the truth that his soul at last experienced, in the gracious face of an adult who mirrored his value, was "It's not your fault." Following this new mediation, Russ and Rusty catch a glimpse of the redeemed fifty-year-old Russ, who is finally able to live an abundant life with authentic relationships.

> Jesus was very, very clear about who he was. That he was beloved by and acceptable to the Father was the most fundamental reality of his identity.

The truth, from a face he trusted, set him free from the lifelong sting of shame he did not need to bear.

Will we listen to the story that hisses lies about our human experiences—that we were responsible for our parents' absence or divorce or death or inability? Will we armor up, protecting ourselves from vulnerability, like Russ? Or will we listen, like Jesus, for the voice that is true? Will we tip our ear toward the voice that says, "You're okay, kid. It's not your fault," and "This is my kid, the beloved, with whom I am well pleased"?

To tip our eyes and ears toward the face and voice that is true is the opportunity that is ours in every moment. In Eugene Peterson's *Message* translation of Jesus's wilderness encounter with the devil, he describes the forty days of fasting as "preparation" for the test. And while it had always seemed to me like being hungry for forty days *was* the test, Peterson's paraphrase opens up the story in a whole new way. If the forty days before encountering the face that lies was preparation, then Jesus prepared for the moments when he would choose between truth and a lie by resting in and marinating in the truth.

Jesus's once-in-a-lifetime wilderness showdown is a template for the kinds of choices we face every day, moment by moment.

Will we tip our ears toward the heavenly voice that announces our once-and-for-all acceptability, or will we bend down toward the voice that lies about who we are? Will we heed the voice that hisses, "You're not *really* God's beloved"?

Because we're *not* privy to the types of visual clues that might tip us off, such as a serpent face or a pitchfork, we can easily be hoodwinked by the tricks of the deceiver. The enemy's deception is subtle, sneaky, and misleading. Sometimes, it can even sound a little bit like the truth! Like the way the serpent hissed to Eve, "Go ahead! Enjoy the fruit. God doesn't really have your back, so you should just take matters into your own hands." Coupled with the lie about our identity—that we're not really God's beloved—is always the suggestion to take things into our own hands. Eat the treat. Reach for the fruit. Turn this stone to bread. Relieve your anxieties with whatever will satisfy.

> To tip our eyes and ears toward the face and voice that is true is the opportunity that is ours in every moment.

And the suggested options always appear more savory than the godly alternative. After all, who wants to say:

I'll bear the pain of loneliness—without reaching for the Ben & Jerry's—because I trust in what the Father provides.

I'll bear the sadness inside me—not reaching for the beer or joint or needle—because I trust in what the Father provides.

I'll stay hungry while I hang on to the truth—not turning to promiscuity.

To agree with the face that is true is to doggedly grip reality.

I'm the Father's.

I'm beloved.

I'm acceptable.

Some of us, like Rusty, believe that we were responsible for our parent's absence or inability to love us in the way we needed to be loved. Like Rusty, being shame-bombed by his dad, the faces that surrounded us convinced us we were other than who we are. Or perhaps the faces that weren't present, like that of Rusty's mother, the ones we *supposed* were unloving, shamed us with their *absence*.

If we are to be free of the sting of shame, that constant low-grade malady from which we've not yet been healed, we must recognize the faces and voices—both real and supposed—that lie.

The earliest faces in our lives have the power to reflect, for us, the truth about who we are or to reflect a lie. In Jesus's experience, his Father whispered, "This is my son, the Beloved, with whom I am well pleased" (Matt. 3:17), and the deceiver hissed something along the lines of, "You're not really who God says you are." Which of these two countenances did the earliest faces in your life most closely resemble? Which is more true?

6

Too Much Lipstick

For the life of me, I don't know how the 2001 movie *A Knight's Tale* has, according to IMDB, only 6.7 stars. It's almost as if . . . voters weren't paying attention. Because this movie is *fantastic*. It is a moving story of identity, the triumph of grace over shame.

The scruffy protagonist, blond-headed William, was raised as a peasant. According to medieval hierarchy: born a peasant, always a peasant. His very birthright was *shameful*. Deeply loved by his father, young William dreamed of altering his destiny by "changing his stars."[1]

As a young adult, William works as a squire—an assistant—for an older knight who traveled the jousting circuit. When his master dies suddenly, William assumes his identity, masquerading as a noble named Ulrich von Lichtenstein, from the fictitious land of Gelderland. The ruse is a roaring success, and "Sir Ulrich" rises through the ranks of jousting knights.

At a tournament in London, William returns to the slum where he'd been raised to find his father, John, whom William assumed to be long dead. He is living, but he has gone blind.

Hearing the approach of footsteps, John inquires, "Who are you?"

William answers, "A knight."

John is familiar with the knight's name, which he's heard being shouted in the nearby stadium. William says he has come to deliver a message: "Your son has changed his stars." As John recognizes his son, the two embrace and weep.

When vindictive Count Adhemar, William's nemesis, discovers his secret, he has him arrested. While William is in jail awaiting his public humiliation in the stocks, Count Adhemar—like the devil taunting Jesus in the wilderness—visits William, shackled and bound. Hissing words of shame, Adhemar punches the helpless man. With each blow, he delivers a stinging assessment.

"You have been weighed."

"You have been measured."

"You have been found wanting."

Striking a final blow, he leaves William battered and bloodied.

The next day, after William is placed in the stocks, one of the hooded guards comes close. Removing the cloak that hides his identity, the "guard" is revealed as none other than Prince Edward. In a previous match, William had, discretely, shown mercy on the prince. Gently approaching him, Edward marvels at how much William's men, still poised by his side, love him. If he knew nothing else of him, the Prince says, *that* would be enough to spare him.

The Prince then orders the guards to release William, and with gratitude for the kindness once shown him, he instructs the released prisoner to kneel. Drawing his sword, the Black Prince of Wales knights the condemned man, proclaiming him not as Sir Ulrich, but *Sir William*.

In an anointing not unlike a riverside baptism dunk or a sanctuary sprinkling, Prince Edward confirms William's true identity.

Though the film is ostensibly about a boy who changes his stars, *making* himself worthy, there is something in the Prince's words to William that suggests otherwise. William is *already* beloved, and the Prince states that this is enough. The faces around him reflect his true worth. Had he not been so *knightly*, had he not been an honorable gentleman, had he not been a talented jouster, and had he not graciously spared the Prince, being beloved would be enough. It's *who he is*.

William's staunch refusal to accept the voices that insisted he was unworthy, and his dogged grip on another reality, form the pattern for him to become who he *really* is.

The Weight of Shame

I'd dropped my boys off for practice before their soccer game and wandered away to find a spot on an empty set of bleachers. The bleachers I chose were empty because families with folding chairs had nestled right next to the soccer field for a better view. Toddlers waddled around with sippy cups, grandparents squinted under sun visors, and siblings poked at each other.

The unskilled six- and seven-year-olds playing on the field seemed worlds away from the proficiency my eleven-year-old boys, practicing on another field, had achieved.

"Kevin!" a woman dressed in jeans, a T-shirt, and baseball cap screeched at one of the players. "Why didn't you stop that?"

Her boy, I calculated, was the goalie who'd just been scored on.

"Pay attention, Kevin!" she shouted, with an angry edge.

When the ball came at him the next time, he stopped it and then kicked it.

When a player from another team intercepted the kick, Kevin's mother, disappointed, hollered, "No, Kevin! NO!"

Her constant harping overpowered all other sounds on the field. The team had an active coach who was encouraging the kids, but he simply could not compete with Tiger Soccer Mom. When he finally called out to have another player switch positions with Kevin, I had to believe it was a gracious decision to take Kevin out of the easy-target glare of the goalie position.

When Kevin didn't switch out of the goalie shirt fast enough, his mother shrieked, "Get that jersey off!"

Her loud, critical voice cast a pall over the whole game.

The face to whom Kevin turned to find out what he was worth said, "You're not good enough."

The Face That Shames

Sometimes the human face that shames is one naturally imbued with authority, like Kevin's mother, and other times it is someone who isn't *authorized* to have a vote in how we see ourselves. Like the brutal Adhemar. It's not a dad or a grandmother or a mentor. And yet, when this person taps into the buried fear we harbor that we're inherently unworthy, it can sting with force.

When my husband and I received a classy invite to the fiftieth birthday of one of my husband's best friends, a tiny seed of dread, which would only blossom and grow over the weeks preceding the party, was planted in my heart. Because I hate parties.

As the eve of the soiree approached, I began to fantasize any number of ways I could end up hospitalized with a broken leg during the big event. Though I've never acted on any of these elaborate violent fantasies, they do sustain me.

The day of the gala, I went shopping for lipstick, mascara, and new hose. Later, at home, I worried about the plethora of other inadequacies that could expose me at the party. These included, but were not limited to, my glasses, earrings, necklace, bracelet, dress, undergarments, and fancy shoes with raggedy heels. After wriggling my way into my costume, carefully waving the magic mascara wand in front of my eyes, and dragging the bright pink lipstick across my mouth, I donned some faux pearl jewelry and at last carefully made my way downstairs.

An eleven-year-old neighbor boy was sitting on the couch playing video games, and he glanced up at me as I clickety-clacked down the stairs.

"MAH-go!" he bellowed, acknowledging my arrival. "Advice?" he demanded. He was asking if I wanted his advice on my appearance. And before I could let him know that I do not take beauty advice from eleven-year-old boys, he barked out his assessment of my appearance.

"TOO MUCH LIPSTICK!"

The fleeting glance and impulsive advice of a boy only confirmed what the sinister voices in my head had been hissing all day long: *You're not quite acceptable the way you are.*

The issue really wasn't even about appearances. The masking and costuming was just an attempt to cover up my dark suspicion that *I* wasn't acceptable as I was.

This is called *shame*, and on the day of my friend's big fancy fiesta, it kicked my butt.

Not All Shaming Faces Are Present Ones

Though it hardly seems fair, we can also internalize shaming faces that are *absent*, ones we can't even see with our eyes. Besides those formative faces we see every day are the ones we long for that have been lost to us.

When my fifth grade teacher was reading to our class from C. S. Lewis's Narnia series—titles like *The Lion, the Witch and the Wardrobe* and *Prince Caspian*—I understood that heroes and heroines Peter, Susan, Edmund, and Lucy were living for a time, without the benefit of parents, in a spacious English countryside estate. Though normally city-dwellers, the Pevensie children went to the country to stay with a remote relation known as "the Professor." This unique circumstance is how they came to discover a magical portal to adventure: a wardrobe that transported them into the mystical land of Narnia. The particular circumstances of their country living did not intrigue me the way the wondrous wardrobe did.

I'm sure our teacher had explained to us that the children had been evacuated from London because of German air raids during World War II. The goal of Britain's "Operation Pied Piper" campaign had been to move 3.5 million vulnerable persons, mostly children, out of populated urban areas such as London, which were expected to be bombed imminently. It was estimated that 1.9 million were actually evacuated.

Posters for the campaign, urging parents to send their children away, identified the target groups for evacuation as school children, mothers of school-aged children, expectant mothers, aged or blind people, and "infirm and invalids." Appealing to parents' innate passion to protect their children, one poster read: "MOTHERS send them out of London . . . give them a chance of greater safety and health." Another, reading "Don't do it, Mother . . . leave the children where they are," seemed to trumpet the opposite message—but became comprehensible when I recognized the wispy silhouette of Adolph Hitler whispering into the mother's ear. The promise was that parents who sent their children away would be keeping them safe from harm. And, in fact, these children were, for the most part, protected from *physical* harm.

Separation Anxieties

Research, however, has revealed that these British children who were *physically* safe in the countryside actually suffered emotionally away from their parents. And those in imminent *physical* danger from the bombings, who remained in close proximity to the face and voice and body of a parent, fared better emotionally in the long haul.

One British psychologist who'd had grave concerns about children being separated from their parents in the mass government effort was John Bowlby. As a pioneer in attachment theory, Bowlby believed that for normal emotional and psychological development to occur, children needed to bond with at least one primary caregiver. The kind of bonding that was requisite wasn't something that could happen then via letters, or even now over Skype: it required physical proximity.

The studies, which were conducted decades after the war ended, confirmed Bowlby's suspicion about the impact of the government's effort. One study interviewed 859 adults (between the ages of sixty-two and seventy-two) who had been evacuated as children.

This study revealed that children who had been between the ages of four and six at the time of separation had sustained significant negative impact. They were at higher risk for depression and clinical anxiety later in life, and were proven to have lower incidences of secure attachment.[2] They also had higher rates of divorce.[3]

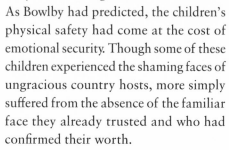

The faces that are conspicuously absent in our lives have the power to form us as much as, and tragically sometimes *more than*, the present ones.

As Bowlby had predicted, the children's physical safety had come at the cost of emotional security. Though some of these children experienced the shaming faces of ungracious country hosts, more simply suffered from the absence of the familiar face they already trusted and who had confirmed their worth.

In the absence of this desired face and without adult assistance to help them understand their feelings, children experience shame.

> If my mother attempted to abort me, it's because I wasn't worth keeping.
>
> If I was abandoned, it's because I wasn't worth sticking around for.
>
> If I was ignored, it's because I wasn't worth nurturing.

A child draws conclusions based on her experience, and believes it to the core. When the reliable daily presence of a parent is lost to death or divorce or incarceration or illness or military service, a child does not know how to process this on her own. Even if her parents sent her away for her own physical safety, the deep imprint of absence is one that forms her.

An Absent Face

When I was in my late twenties, my birthfather and I connected once, by letter, and he was not interested in further contact.

Outwardly, I acted brave, even feigning compassion. Because I'd barged into his life, I'd narrate to others, I completely understood why he didn't want to see me. But despite the courageous mask I wore, my deep longings to be seen and received squeaked out of me as I slept. In my dreams, I would recognize Max, my birthfather, on a crowded New York City street. Against all odds, I would pick him out as my own. He would then see me and recognize me as his own and take me home to care for me, like a lost puppy.

These dreams infuriated me. A needy puppy is not how I saw myself in my waking hours, and it was not who I wanted to be. I wanted to be the strong, smiling, confident happy-mask I showed everyone else.

That my birthfather had chosen, a second time, to not want me stung.

Faces that shame are not just the ones that are *present*, raging at soccer games, belittling at the dinner table, or degrading on report card day. To be left, rejected, or abandoned; sent away to safety, to the hospital, or to school; or even adopted into a good-enough home is, for many, to be shamed by *a face that isn't even there*!

The faces that are conspicuously absent in our lives have the power to form us as much as, and tragically sometimes *more than*, the present ones.

Weighed, Measured, and Found Wanting

Jonathan's mother was erratic, unpredictable, and capricious. When he'd come home from school each day, he could not anticipate whether she would be knitting him a scarf or wildly wielding knives. She could be laughing at a television show or weeping in her bedroom. Because *she* was unable to receive him, he feared that he was not worthy of being received by *anyone*.

At the root of shame is a very primal anxiety: if we're not accepted by others, we fear we will be left alone. Unworthy of love, we'll be abandoned, entirely, by all. Whether conscious, or more often subconscious, it is a terrifying possibility for any child or adult.

Lewis Smedes explains this fear.

To be disgraceful is to be weighed and found unacceptable to those whom we need most to accept us. It is, in short, to be despised and rejected by our own. Is this not the shame we all fear most? Is it not the *primal* shame that we dread more than death itself?[4]

As our brains were being knit together in early childhood, when we did not have the skills to meet our own daily needs, to have been rejected would have meant actual physical death. Though no longer useful, our early programming continues to hum in our circuits.

A child, egocentric, naturally assumes he deserves whatever is doled out. So if someone shames him—by his absence or by his presence, with her face or with her words—a child needs help to interpret and to understand that, no matter what's been endured, he is not shameful.

Peasant William, whom the world did not expect to come to very much, *had* that adult helper in his father. When John had planted a little seedling about changing his stars in the heart of his young son, William learned that his value was not determined by the faces around him. He learned that he was *worthy*.

Shame says that we are not quite acceptable the way we are. Whether that message was spoken to us or whether we pieced it together from our circumstances—from present faces and absent ones—it is a lie. Ask God to help you release any face that failed to reflect your inherent worth.

We Mask Up to Cover Shame

Driven by the fear of being rejected by those whom we most need to accept us, we learn to hide who we really are. Donning masks, we present the image to others that we are a little bit better than we actually are. Both shame and all the posing we do to hide it interfere with our relationships with others and with God.

7

Spidey's Getting the Love

What you see with me is what you get.

Sort of.

When folks I've just met are effusively flattering with me—perhaps after I've tried to sound as smart as I can, or as funny as I can, or as perceptive as I can, or as spiritual as I can—I often recognize a common refrain in their comments. While I wish it were otherwise, they're never remarking how smart or funny or perceptive or spiritual I am.

More often, wearing the kind of expression you might notice on someone who's just experienced something really horrible while changing a baby's diaper, they'll observe, "You're so . . . *real*." Their faces clearly indicate that while they're really glad that *I'm* this thing, it's not necessarily something to which they aspire. So it's great that someone else is doing it.

Perhaps I've just shared an incredibly insightful quote I recently gleaned, not from reading a book but from the signature line of a smart person's email signature. Or maybe I've tossed off a line that got my husband a few laughs last week. Or maybe I've gotten lucky and have said something that's perceived as wise. Or, despite the fact that I'm currently living in a dry spiritual wasteland, I could be sharing a brilliant spiritual insight I gleaned twelve years ago.

But because I will sometimes use the word "fart," even admitting on rare occasion to executing one, or because I mention that I survive because of antidepressants, or admit that I do not own a brush or a comb, people get this idea in their heads that I am *real*. And in the classic *Velveteen Rabbit* sense of realness—because I've been through the wringer a bit, my fur is raggedy and my tail has fallen off and I have just one plastic eye—I suppose I am, *technically*, real.

But let me assure you that I am usually trying *really hard* to appear way better than I am.

People often fail to recognize that.

And while I appreciate the props, the truth of the situation more often than not is that I'd meant to look better, but failed.

I Really Try

I try to appear better than I am *all the time*.

Last week I was holed up in a remote hotel for two days, writing. As a result of forces outside my control— namely, my daughter destroying my MacBook's touchpad by spilling a cup of water on it—I am now forced to carry around a wireless mouse everywhere my laptop goes. When I arrive at a destination mouse-less, I am simply out of luck. My luck, last week, was not fantastic.

Though I did manage to arrive at the hotel with mouse in hand, I was only a few hours into working when its batteries died. I was desperate to be writing, and without any backup batteries in my laptop case, it felt rather disastrous. My hotel was in a remote, scary office park and I had no idea how to reach civilization, let alone find batteries.

So I did what any reasonable person would do: I hijacked the batteries from the television remote. I'd seen my video game–addicted, controller-wielding children do it a million times.

And because I wanted to watch TV for a few minutes while I snacked, and then when I ate dinner, and then later when I snacked again, my situation dissolved into a rather ridiculous repetitive routine.

As one might imagine, I succeeded in draining every ounce of power out of those batteries. It was after eleven at night when I went to the front desk, remote in hand, in search of new batteries.

"Do you have extra AA batteries?" I asked, purposefully trying to keep my voice from revealing my deceit.

I acted like some poor traveler who just wanted to watch *Nancy Grace* in peace and had to come all the way downstairs. Sort of like the hotel had inconvenienced me a little bit.

"Hmmm . . . not sure if we do. Let me check . . ."

This was followed by an elaborate ritual of battery testing in the remote, and concluded with the offer to give me a new room if the remote did not, in fact, work.

The "new room" thing made me think the closest convenience store carrying batteries must have been even farther away than I had calculated.

"Oh no, don't do that." I backpedaled. "I know how to *stand up* and turn a channel. I'm *that* old."

The entire ruse depended upon me pretending that I was *not* one of those people who tries to cheat hotels out of batteries. I

> The truth of the situation more often than not is that I'd meant to look better, but failed.

didn't *purpose* to mask up in order to communicate to a complete stranger that I was better than the battery-stealing thief I really was.

In fact, such masking seems to be first-nature. Without even realizing it, I work to appear as though I'm a little bit more put-together than I actually am.

How I Am

When Megan, the kind dental hygienist, asks if I've been flossing, I'll mumble something like, "I do not floss often." And, of course, what I mean by that is, "I have not flossed in the last six months since you flossed my teeth *for* me."

When I blog about the evils of "Stuffmart"—thank you to the creators of VeggieTales for that euphemism—then I feel like I'm not, technically, a hypocrite for shopping at Walmart. Because, technically, I'm not shopping at a fictional place called . . . Stuffmart.

When I call the school office to explain why my son, who is home being treated for head lice, is not present, I'll say he's "sick." So that whoever answers the phone doesn't think we're one of *those* families.

My default setting is to mask up. What keeps me in most every moment from being who I really am is the fear that I'll be weighed, measured, and found wanting. So, without ever purposing to, I mask.

These masks, the ones I can point to and describe and touch, are *featherweight* compared to the constricting and unflinching one I wore for more than twenty-five years. That one was welded so tightly to my person that I could not see it or know it to be *other* than me, and it had all the more power *because* I did not recognize it. For all those years I simply assumed that the face that smiled back at me in the mirror was my own.

Instead of receiving the love intended for us, the *mask* receives it. Like being protected from the rain by one of those ridiculous umbrella-hats, when we stick out our tongue to taste the rain, we remain parched.

Frank Lake described my bind when he wrote, "We prefer to be known by our mask while there is any reasonable chance of being able to maintain it successfully in the public eye."[1] Had I been able to maintain my mask, there's no question I would have chosen to keep it. What happened, instead, is that the pain and fear and sadness long buried in my heart began to leak out. And, as it did, that leaky acid began to corrode the mask that had protected me from facing what had been safely buried away in my deepest place.

Best thing that ever happened to me.

Though at the time it felt excruciating, it was, for me, the way to life. In fact, I've become convinced that heading straight into the heart of conflict is the unlikely path to freedom from it. On the other side now, no longer a slave to avoiding what's real, I feel like that mangy *Velveteen Rabbit*. When that critter was smooth and shiny and new, he wasn't quite real. I wasn't either. But through the process of having my fur rubbed off, my shell cracked, and my mask removed, I became real.

I know I did not make that sound very savory, but it is truly the *way* to life.

The Lie

Authors John Lynch, Bill Thrall, and Bruce McNicol confirm that the biggest problem living *masked* is that, when authentic love does come our way, we're "protected" from receiving it! Instead of receiving the love intended for us, the *mask* receives it. Like being protected from the rain by one of those ridiculous umbrella-hats, when we stick out our tongue to taste the rain, we remain parched.

Imagine it's Halloween and your four-year-old is dressed up in a squishy, fake-muscled, spandex Spiderman costume. Friends and neighbors see him and say, "Spiderman is awesome! Look at you. You're *so* strong! Yay Spidey!" And for a moment your child feels fantastic. Eventually, though, bedtime comes. The costume comes off. He looks in the mirror and realizes, once again, that he's a small and relatively weak boy. And in some corner of his heart he's entirely aware that the comments declaring him acceptable and worthy weren't really about him at all.

Deep down, he understands that when a costume stood between him and everyone else, and even impressed adoring others, it was the *costume* that got the love and adulation. What he knows intuitively, but cannot articulate, is that the frail awkward boy inside the super suit was never *really* seen or known or affirmed. People were responding to the *costume* and not the boy. And in his deepest places, he may fear that the *boy* is not enough.

Adults are no different. In order to protect ourselves, we deny others access to our true selves by allowing them to see only the masks we've chosen. These masks suggest that we've really got our acts together. But at the end of the day, we're left feeling pretty alone.

The tragic result is that others never *really* come to know who we are on the inside. Sure, they'll praise us for our amazing scrapbooks, or hand-knit Christmas stockings, or clever parenting strategies, or even our eloquent prayers. But the person we are on the inside—the one we think is such a mess—never gets *loved* because when there's a mask between us and others, it's our *masks* that end up receiving the love others freely offer. It's like having a refreshing water gun fight on a hot, hot day while wearing a thick rubber scuba suit and diving mask. When it's the mask and rubber suit that receive the mist or the spray or the love or the grace, our insides remain unrefreshed.

The deep sadness is that if we never allow others to see inside, if we even fool ourselves into believing that the masks are who we really are, then our deep human longing to be fully known for who we are—and loved anyway!—can never be met. And because we've been so thoroughly conditioned to keep up appearances, like frogs in a slowly heating pot of water, we don't even have the good sense to be alarmed.

This was never the plan of the One who loves us.

Whose Plan?

Let's say that it's October 31. You're just opening the first bag of fun size candy and the kids, gripping little orange plastic flashlights, have donned their outfits and are itchy to hit the pavement.

Before clicking off the evening news, you hear the news anchor describe a nationwide recall of a particular lot of children's Halloween costumes. She explains that materials used by a certain manufacturer overseas are actually very toxic and should be returned to the store for proper disposal. When the well-groomed anchor mentions a few major retailers, you grab the closest pen and scribble the information she gives onto the closest junk mail envelope.

When you're finally able to catch hold of your little superhero, reach into his outfit, and read the lot number on his garment tag, you realize that the costume you've bought came from a *bad* batch. The fact only confirms your nagging suspicion that you're a *bad mom* for buying a costume from a big box retailer in the first place—instead of stitching an exact replica of your child's *Raggedy Andy* doll like your wholesome homeschooling neighbor has done.

Because you have no compensatory bribe in hand to wedge your child *out* of the death-dealing costume, you suddenly realize there is only one way forward; you will peel it off of him, slather him in antibacterial soap, and hose him down in the backyard. Then you will wrap him in tinfoil and tell him he's the Tin Man from the *Wizard of Oz*.

When the mask and costume your child is wearing is harming him, you have the good sense to remove it immediately, regardless of the ensuing drama.

Reticent to Unmask

We don't always exercise the same sensibility when we're the ones wearing the suffocating, toxic costume.

Like me, too many of us have believed that if others knew who we *really* were—people who yell and overspend and criticize our partners more than we mean to—we'd be left alone. Often unaware, longing for acceptance, we've worn masks to preserve the appearance that we're someone other than who we really are. And though the masks and teeny lies have seemed harmless enough— fudging on our weight, or keeping our addictions behind closed doors, or giving the silent impression that we're not struggling financially—these masks we've used to convince others that we're worth knowing and loving have actually *prevented* us from receiving the love we're after.

"What? What's that, now? I thought it was the other way around!"

I know; it's completely counterintuitive, right?

The promise of the mask is that people will love us more with it. We wear it to protect ourselves from the sting of rejection, never once realizing that these suffocators are actually keeping us from what we most long for.

Handed to us by the enemy, these toxic masks keep us breathing recycled shame. They also reinforce the shame of others around us who are mistakenly led to believe we've got our stuff together. The ruse that we're better than we actually are adds to *their* shame! The masks *parents* wear not only confuse our children, who *know* better than anyone what's beneath them, but they also send the clear message to our daughters and sons that it's simply too risky to let others see who you really are.

This was *never* the plan of the One who loves you. Instead, the sinister message, which has effectively convinced us to cover up, is a lie of the deceiver. It's like that World War II poster with Hitler hissing in a mother's ear. With it, the enemy of our souls, who gave us the idea for the mask in the first place, keeps us tangled up in shame and prevents us from discovering the truth. God is never the one who encourages us to mask, to pose, to feign, or to pretend. Rather, when we reveal who we really are in a safe space—to ourselves, to God, and to others—we realize that we are not loved *less* but rather are loved *more*.

Living Mask-Free

For some of us, the invitation to live mask-free actually feels more like living *skin*-free. That's certainly how I felt during the difficult season when my own mask was deteriorating. When the disguises we've worn for so long have fused right to us, the thought of removing them can feel absolutely terrifying.

Our terror begs the question, "If you were to actually encounter someone who—confident that they were accepted by God exactly as they were—was living entirely without masks, would you even *recognize* them?"

Well, for starters, they wouldn't be without skin. They'd have skin that could stretch up into a smile, and furrow between angry brows, and raise those eyebrows in surprise. What differentiates the mask-free person from the rest of us is that the face on the outside doesn't *disguise* what's inside, it *reveals* it. Instead of a sad person wearing a false grin, or a fearful person bursting out in an angry rage, the unmasked person presents herself to others as she really is.

The unmasked person is so completely comfortable accepting all that he is—the good, the bad, and the ugly—that there's no need to present a false façade to others.

I think the mask-free person might look a bit like one of my friends with intellectual disabilities, in that she wouldn't pose to impress. She'd be comfortable interacting with others exactly as they are.

I think the person living so free might offend some folks. Without the desperate need to feign humility or couch his real opinions so that others continue to like him or appear a little bigger than he actually is, this one would probably speak quite bluntly.

> **Handed to us by the enemy, these toxic masks keep us breathing recycled shame.**

The unmasked person would be a bit childlike, the wonderful kind of childlike that has no need to be constantly evaluating how others might be evaluating her. At cocktail parties she'd say completely unpretentious things like, "I really don't enjoy reading that much. I'd much rather watch a reality show on television." I feel certain she'd be terribly unimpressive.

If you've seen the sitcom *Raising Hope*, living unmasked is a bit like Jimmy's parents, Burt and Virginia. Sure, sometimes these poor, simple folks will break into a fancy home, pretending it's their own, to convince out-of-state relatives that they've done well for themselves. But when Burt and Virginia pose, they *know* they're posing. More often they're ridiculously genuine.

When the maskless person fills out his height and weight on a driver's license, he writes his exact weight, that day, not the weight he intends to be a few months down the line when he gets pulled over.

The unmasked person is like the fabulous character Fat Amy in the 2012 comedy *Pitch Perfect*. Overweight, laughable at times, Fat Amy gives no indication that she wants, in any way, to be anything *other than exactly how she is.*

• • • • •

Grace does not *erase* who you are. It's not putting a shiny coat of Jesus-paint over a horribly mildewed and rotting wall. It means, instead, that all that you are is known by God— and received in full.

• • • • •

The person living mask-free would be unashamedly transparent, exactly as he is, with no need to hide what was inside him to impress those outside him. Confident he was accepted by God, he'd accept himself entirely.

Doesn't this sound like a great way to live?

Risky Business

If you're like I was for years, this whole business makes you a little nervous.

Admittedly, it's risky, right? Because what if you dare to remove your protective mask and end up getting hurt or rejected? Even when it's not conscious, the deep fear of being rejected and abandoned drives our mask-wearing.

Before you try going mask-free at a cocktail party, consider doing it before God.

Let me be clear: what I don't mean by that is that you approach God under cover of the Jesus shield. Too often we've believed, *When God looks at me he sees Jesus, because I'm too gross to look at. Good thing Jesus is shielding me from God!* Nothing about going to God while dragging a huge load of shame with you is good news!

Some of us have gotten tangled up in this bind. Because the Scriptures do affirm that we are "covered" by the righteous blood of Jesus, we assume our very identity has been cloaked and hidden when Jesus stands between us and the Father. In fact, those of us who want to be intimately known and loved by God can be left feeling lonely if we believe that, in our redemption, we've been generically sanitized, scrubbed free both of sin and all that makes us uniquely ourselves. This is the threat a child of color might feel when promised in Sunday School that, clean from sin, she'll be made "white as snow." No! This isn't *that* kind of "covering." Jesus's sacrifice *for* us is more like the moment in the restaurant when it's time to pay the bill and you realize your wallet is at home. When Jesus says, "No problem, I've got it covered," you experience being *more* known and loved, not less. Grace does not *erase* who you are. It's not putting a shiny coat of Jesus-paint over a horribly mildewed and rotting wall. It means, instead, that all that you are is known by God—and received in full.

My friend Jeff has helped me appreciate this. He delights in the fact that God has given us a face-to-face relationship with himself. Because of God's grace, Jeff reminds me, we can come boldly to God without shame. We don't cower behind Jesus because we're so filthy. Rather, because of Jesus's work on our behalf, God sees the real us, as we are, and accepts us. God receives us exactly as we are. In the language of Frank Lake, "The eyes of a holy Love . . . look upon this wretchedness and really see it, and in spite of what it sees, go on looking in kindliness and welcome."[2]

That, right there, is the deep longing of each heart: for the eyes of Love to really see us, and to continue to gaze upon us in kindliness anyway. When we internalize *these* eyes, we're set free to lose the masks and be who we really are.

This face that sees us as we are, and goes on looking in kindliness and welcome, is the face of the One for whom we long.

The Surprise

A few years ago I heard John Lynch, one of the authors of *Truefaced*, speaking at a Hungry for Hope conference in Colorado

Springs. His message, one I had no idea that I'd been desperately thirsting for, just filled me up. What I heard from him was something like this: "When we dare to take off the mask, and let people see who we really are, we find not that we are loved less, but that we are loved more!"

Though at first blush this seemed both unlikely and terrifying, I knew it immediately to be true.

John had found it to be true in a group of guys who'd loved him well. It certainly rang true from my own experience. During the twenty-five years I was living masked-up, I was not receiving any of the love that others offered to me. When welcomed, I felt rejected. When received, I felt abandoned. When remembered, I felt forgotten. It was for me, and possibly for those around me, *brutal*.

When my smiley mask came off, though—against my will—those around me saw who I really was. I was emotionally unable to smile, with years of stunted tears bursting forth, no longer able to mask up even when I tried—and the care of others was finally reaching the real *me*.

The enemy's lie is that if people knew who we really were, they'd reject us. It's the constant gnawing fear with which we live. The God-honest truth that not too many folks are talking about is that the way to life is the path that feels like death. Those who are brave enough to give it a try, to lower the mask that insists we're other than who we are, are discovering this glorious surprise.

We lower the mask with ourselves.

We lower it in the presence of others.

We lower it in the presence of God.

I don't suspect there is any particular sequence, among the three, to this complete authenticity into which we're invited. Again, I think it's chicken-and-eggy. Lowering one mask facilitates the crumbling of others. I *do* know what girds and protects us when we dare to try. It is the assurance that we are, despite the hiss of the enemy that says otherwise, entirely accepted by God exactly as we are.

When we know that to be true in our bones, when we really own it for ourselves, we are empowered to live free in the presence of all others.

Are there ways in which you "mask up" to present yourself to others as being "better" than you actually are? How do you do it? This week, commit to allowing others to see you as you really are. Maybe you will go makeup-free. Maybe you'll confess a weakness to a friend. Maybe you'll stop yourself when tempted to make yourself out to be just a wee bit better than you are. How will you lower the mask, even just a bit, for others to see the real you?

8

Because We're Not
Land Snails

ecently Dr. Timothy Johnson, a passionate ABC news corre-
spondent, reported in earnest, "Now, a *new* study finds that
for *all* women, wearing makeup significantly changes how they
are perceived."[1]

Perhaps if you say anything with earnest excitement it becomes
newsworthy? I thought we all agreed that this is how we are already
operating. Apparently this new study found that the *more* makeup
a woman used, the more she was judged to be attractive, likeable,
trustworthy, and competent.

And this is a surprise?

I'm thinking it was a slow news day.

Of *course* women are judged more favorably when we wear
makeup. Our culture's preference for women to be made up,
masked, and hiding our actual faces is the way it works. In response
to the eyes of others, we've masked up appropriately.

Men, here's a peek into our heads: another study reported that
two-thirds of women believed that going to work makeup-free was

more stressful than public speaking, a job interview, or a first date.[2] Ninety-one percent of women said they'd rather cancel a first date than go without makeup. The reason all those things are stressful in the first place—dating, interviewing, speaking publicly—is because, in each, we're being evaluated. The eyes on us are deciding if we're worth hearing, worth hiring, or worth knowing.

When asked, few women are willing to attribute our "preference" to be seen with makeup to any innate hunger for acceptance. We don't like to say we fear the judgment of others. In fact, we'll go to great lengths to insist just the opposite.

"I feel more confident and 'refreshed' with makeup on."

"It's about personal preference."

"I enjoy putting makeup on."

"I feel more awake and ready for the day."

"I love makeup, it makes me feel good."

"I wear it for me."

We'll bend over backward to be clear that we're *not* doing this for the eyes of others. We don't care what other people think of us, we insist. We do it for ourselves.

Were we land snails, I might find this rationale convincing. If we had long eye tentacles that bent so that we could see ourselves at our desks or grocery shopping or exercising, I might buy it. I might believe that we were really wearing makeup *for ourselves*. But, since we can't actually see our own faces outside the moments we glance into mirrors, I find the excuses weak.

As a little reality check, if everyone you were going to encounter today was blind, would you still need to wear makeup? I can already hear the diehards protesting, "I'd still wear makeup if everyone on the planet was blind! I'd wear it because *I* love wiping sticky goo on myself! I'd do it if *I* was blind and everybody else was blind. Because I love goo and it makes me feel good to be sticky!"

Fine. Whatever.

But ask any truth-telling makeup-wearing woman how it feels to be caught makeup-free—by an early morning knock at the door, or a rush-out-of-the house emergency—and she'll tell you that it is *not* comfortable. Most of us are keenly aware of others' perceptions of us and we *do* prefer to be seen—even by the gas station attendant from whom we're buying emergency tampons—as attractive, likeable, trustworthy, and competent. All of those would certainly be my personal preferences.

Oh, Margot, you might be thinking, *does it really come down to cosmetics?*

No, no.

So many women's made-up faces just happen to be an apt symbol for the ways women and men cover our faces, disguising who we really are, to be more acceptable to others.

In our Christmas letters, we naturally show people the side of our families that puts us in the best light. Or we at least show them the angles of which we're most proud.

When it benefits us, when we think it serves us well, we behave as if our jobs, our careers, are going a little better than they actually are.

When our doctor asks us how often we exercise, we offer an estimate that's a wee bit more than we actually do. We keep it close enough so that we're not lying *a lot*, but it's also not accurate.

When we have to write down our weight when being issued sporting equipment, like skis or hang gliders, we fudge a little. Even if it might kill us.

We make ourselves look a little better than we actually are, in the hope that we might be well-received by others. Whether we are or not is debatable.

More Real and Less Real

Though it's first-nature for me to put on my happy-mask for church, and my intelligent-mask at the academy, and my attempt-at-witty-mask when posting on Facebook, I *know* what it is to live mask-less.

For better or for worse, the people with whom I share meals and television screens and toilets do too. The ones I allow to experience me completely unedited—though at times editing how I am would be advisable—are my family members. Confident that none of them are leaving anytime soon, though one or two might be counting the days until college orientation, I give them the privilege of seeing who I really am. And for that, my precious children, I apologize. I fume. I rage. Sometimes I belch. I have lots of other authentic facial expressions too—the post-belch-laugh face, and the proud my-kid-just-made-a-goal face, and the hooray-you-swept-the-floor face—that don't need to be masked as much as the ones that put me in a bad light.

But if I'm given the opportunity to meet some D-list celebrity—a writer, a speaker, an agent, an actor, a politician—someone I've admired from a distance and have fortuitously just had the chance to meet in person, you can bet I'm going to mask up. I'll use every disguise in my costume chest to appear more warm, intelligent, and funny than I naturally am. I'm not pretending this works. I usually get nervous and say something stupid or forget my name, but I try. I try as hard as I can to be someone other than who I am.

But then, on the off chance someone I admire loves me back, maybe because they know my writing or speaking, I discount the love with the ominous thought, *They don't know. They don't know how I really am. If they knew, they probably wouldn't care much for me at all.*

It's completely sinister.

But the flipside is also true: I really do receive love that is authentic from the folks with whom I am—though it isn't always pretty—*most real.* My kids. My husband. A few reliable friends. All my parents. They have seen who I really am and the love that comes from them is the real deal.

Though a lot of us wouldn't choose unmasking to allow others to see who we really are, it is a choice to lower the shame-shield,

> **Though a lot of us wouldn't choose unmasking to allow others to see who we really are, it is a choice to lower the shame-shield, to disagree with the lie that we're not worth loving, and to see what happens.**

to disagree with the lie that we're not worth loving, and to see what happens.

Sometimes, we get the love we're actually after.

A Tragic Refusal to Be Loved

Cyrano de Bergerac is a nobleman serving as a soldier in the French army. Clever with words, he's a talented poet. Gifted with instruments, he's a skilled musician. Handy with a sword, he's a duelist. He's also a *dualist*. Ashamed of his very large nose, a source of great insecurity for him, he hides his affection for Roxanne and helps Christian, another suitor, win Roxanne's heart.

The ruse begins innocently when Cyrano helps handsome Christian write a letter to Roxanne. When she begins to recognize a discrepancy between the eloquent pen-wielder and the bumbling, live man, Cyrano jumps in again to put words in Christian's mouth. Roxanne and Christian are wed and, before they can share even one night together, he is sent off to the front lines of battle. When Roxanne begs Cyrano to make Christian write her every day, Cyrano—grateful for the opportunity to express his affection for his beloved—gladly agrees and writes her faithfully, twice a day, throughout the war.

Desperate to see her beloved, Roxanne flirts her way to the battlefield, confiding in Christian that she has grown to love him through the letters, and that she'd love him even if he were ugly. What might be an assurance for another man came as a devastating blow to Christian as he realized that it was not he that she loved, but Cyrano. Confiding in his friend Cyrano, Christian reveals, "I will be loved myself—or not at all!" Christian, "masked" by the voice of Cyrano, cannot receive the love Roxanne offers because he knows it is not for him.

Though Christian urges Cyrano to drop *his* mask, to show his true face to Roxanne, bound by fear and insecurity, de Bergerac refuses. Pretending he had confided in Roxanne, Cyrano even assures Christian, on his deathbed, that Roxanne, aware of the truth, still loves Christian.

Fourteen years later, Roxanne is living in a convent outside Paris where she continues to mourn Christian. Cyrano visits her regularly, as a friend, with the day's news. One day, having suffered a head injury, he arrives and is clearly dying. Knowing it will be his last visit, he asks if he can read Christian's farewell letter, which she carries at her breast. Roxanne gladly offers it to him to read aloud. As he speaks the words born of his own heart, she recognizes in them the voice that belongs to Cyrano. When he continues to "read" after it's become too dark to read, she sees at last.

" 'Twas you!" Roxanne exclaims.

"No, never," Cyrano denies, "Roxanne, no!"

She protests, suddenly acknowledging the hollowness of Christian's mask, "I should have guessed, each time he said my name!"

Cyrano retorts, "No, it was not I!"

The back-and-forth goes on. Ten times Roxanne recognizes Cyrano as the love behind the letters. Ten times he denies it. His final denial reveals a crack in his armor, "No, my sweet love, I never loved you!"

At last seeing through his ruse, the final question that lingers on her lips is, "Why?" Why had he remained silent?

Cyrano could not answer.

As he begins to die, Roxanne protests, "Live, for I love you!"

Still, he protests, "No, in fairy tales, when to the ill-starred Prince the lady says 'I love you!' all his ugliness fades fast—but I remain the same, up to the last!"

The story to which he clings is the story of *The Princess and the Frog*.

"I've marred your life," Roxanne gasps, in horror. She believes herself to have been complicit in the very primal story Cyrano has believed and to which he has clung.

"You blessed my life! Never on me had rested woman's love. My mother even could not find me fair: I had no sister; and, when a grown man, I feared the mistress who would mock at me. But I have had your friendship—grace to you a woman's charm has passed across my path."[3]

In his final words, the source of his pain is revealed: that his mother never found him fair. Having internalized her shaming eyes, he was, until the end, unable to receive the gaze of love from another.

Cyrano's story is our story. He masked up, taking the face of dashing Christian, believing it the only way to be received by Roxanne. The tragedy, of course, is that neither Christian nor Cyrano received the love for which they longed. Both went to death unloved.

The lie Cyrano believed is the same one we've believed: if people see who we really are, we'll be unloved. Admittedly, it's a risk to drop the masks we wear, to practice authenticity. So, afraid, we mask up.

What's a sure thing, though, is that when we allow others to see only the masks, our needs will *not* be met.

Only when we've dropped the masks do we allow the possibility of receiving the kind of acceptance-without-condition we crave in our deep places. To practice authenticity requires courage.

Hammering the Pharisees

When Jesus really laid into the Pharisees and experts in the law, it was about this very thing. It was about wearing masks.

In Luke's telling, it started when Jesus reclined at the table without performing a ceremonial washing first. Keenly aware he was breaking custom, Jesus pushes the envelope by then describing how the Pharisees were clean on the outside and dirty on the inside. Specifically, he detailed the ways they loved to be seen in the important seats in the synagogues and to be greeted respectfully in the marketplace. They wore masks so that they might be perceived well by others (Luke 11:37–54).

Jesus's transparent assessment of the condition of their hearts naturally evoked a response. The Pharisees and experts in the law opposed him and besieged him with angry questions. And while, over the centuries, we've grown accustomed to caricaturing them in this way, it wasn't the only response they might have chosen.

Others, in Jesus's presence, chose *not* to mask up further, *not* to cover up and hide, but to confess who they really were: a Samaritan woman at a well, a tax collector named Zacchaeus on a crowded street, a sinful man who went to the temple to pray. When their masks came down, they were at last able to receive acceptance and welcome.

Courage to Be Real

The invitation is one that is extended to us as well. As those who've moved through life with a shine on the outside and shame on the inside, we live into freedom when we choose to live authentically. When we let folks see our smudges and stains, we agree with the truth: that we are beloved despite them. The surprising reversal—which feels counterintuitive—is evident in Jesus's story of the Pharisee and the reputed sinner who went to the temple to pray. Though one might expect the shiny-exterior Pharisee to be justified, it is, rather, the one who reveals *who he really is* who goes home justified.

> What's a sure thing, though, is that when we allow others to see only the masks, our needs will *not* be met.

To view Jesus's engagement with the Pharisees as a plea for them to finally drop the masks of Religious rightness is to recognize it as an overwhelmingly loving act. Knowing how they were, Jesus also knew that they would be unable to receive God's love for them as long as they wore the costumes of whitewashed tomb and squeaky clean dish. Only when they came to God as they really were would they receive God's grace and mercy.

To be clear, God wasn't holding out on them. God wasn't keeping back a good gift. Rather, he wanted them to know that they couldn't wear a full-body scuba suit into the shower and expect to come out clean. To be justified, to be cleansed, to be received, they needed to get a little bit naked, coming to God as they were.

The invitation to those good-on-the-outside Pharisees is the same one extended to you and me.

As we take baby steps to be real with others and to be real with God, we're finally positioned to receive the love and grace that is so freely showered upon us.

If we are to allow others to see our true faces, we must be able to see them ourselves! Just as we avoid unmasking in front of others, so too we even avoid being real with God and ourselves. Take time to be still with God and allow him to show you parts of yourself you typically avoid. Be willing to sit with these—with your shame or guilt or hurts or fears—and allow them to simply **be** in God's gracious presence.

9

Supermom Made Her Kid Cry

Not long after we'd met, I'd pegged Tina as one of those supermoms. For starters, there was no clear evidence that she ever lost her temper. Nothing makes me madder than these non-angry mothers. My suspicions were confirmed one evening in her kitchen when one of her children, frustrated, threw a spoonful of her homemade spaghetti sauce across the kitchen. Cowering, I waited for the kind of uncontrolled angry maternal blast with which *I* might have exploded under the same circumstances. None came. Instead, Tina just merrily continued pumping her salad spinner.

Tina was also of that ilk of mothers that apparently had nothing better to do—like losing their tempers—than to expose her children to culture of all varieties. And I do not mean Leonardo and Michelangelo of the *Teenage Mutant Ninja Turtles*. If she wasn't loading up the van to shuttle those kids to a museum in a neighboring city, she was standing in line for discount tickets to musical theater. She even took one of her children on a field trip to the Louvre. The one in Paris.

And though I had no empirical evidence to prove it, I'd also stereotyped her as the virtuous type of mother who would curl up under the covers to read a different story to *each* of her three children instead of corralling them into a large open space, like I did with mine, and reading into a bullhorn. Again, I never actually witnessed this, but I had just enough unfounded inklings to make an uneducated guess.

In case it's not clear, Tina—and her supermom ilk—really get on my last nerve.

These Supermoms

When these women congregate at our local park while our kids waddle and slide and lose pricey sippy cups, there will be the rare occasion when one of the supermoms will be hot, hungry, and tired enough to let some *truth* spill out. No one's quite deranged enough to admit the *big* truth—that they spank too hard or sneak-smoke or drink too much or hate their mothers-in-law—but when their resources are compromised they'll let *little* truths slip.

One confesses to letting her child watch *two* episodes of *Clifford* so she could finish stitching her daughter a homemade dress and matching bonnet for Easter. Another admits to giving her toddler an M&M while she snapped a quick picture for one of the nineteen Creative Memories scrapbooks she's designed for each month of his short little life. Another sheepishly confesses that she let her child's friend sleep over on the *same sheets* her in-laws had used the week before so that she wouldn't have to wash and *iron* them again.

That these are the best confessions my friends can muster is more than a little disappointing.

So at the playground or the pool or the church nursery, when Tina confesses that she's "lost it" with her kids, I don't ever believe her. It is simply inconceivable to me that someone who can nonchalantly shrug off red, flying kitchen liquid could ever approximate anything close to what I consider "losing it." Certainly not when I *purposely* employ the euphemism to *disguise* whatever embarrassing offense I've most recently committed against humanity.

For example, if while raging against my children, I've shot them a scowl of pure evil—where lightning bolts that rip through their squishy little souls shoot out of my eyes—I might later tell another mom like Tina that I "lost it."

Or maybe I've asked my offspring to pick up their socks and blankets off the floor twenty-nine times, and they're still raucously wrestling in our oversized beanbags. When I respond by screaming so hard that my throat still hurts the next morning, I'll sheepishly tell women in my Bible study that I "lost it."

> I do it so that I won't give anyone close to me reason to reject me or leave me. I do it so I won't be alone.

If I have become so enraged at one of my little angels that I *chase* after him as he's angrily stomping up the stairs so that I can smack his butt on the way up, I'll call my husband and confess that "I *really* lost it."

I think this is why I don't take Supermom Tina's confession of "losing it" very seriously. I'm so convinced that she is a better breed of mother, wife, and human being than I am that I can't really believe she's as bad as I am.

I think I also doubt her because I'm slowly becoming aware that when *I* tell other women that I "lost it," I'm not telling the *whole* truth. Though I convey the appearance of transparency, I'm *still* saving face. I'm gleaning some of the cathartic benefits of confession while never troubling others with the whole *ugly* truth about me. I'm not telling them that, completely unglued, I poured a glass of water over the head of my undone two-year-old. Unchecked, it's how I operate. Without ever intending to deceive, most certainly not while feigning authenticity, I present the image to others that I'm a teeny bit more loving or patient or kind than I actually am. I preserve the appearance that I've got my act mostly together. In moments of accidental self-awareness, I realize that I do it so that I won't give anyone close to me reason to reject me or leave me. I do it so I won't be alone.

Confession

SuperTina had been reading a book at the pool when she set it down in her lap and looked off into the distance. Turning to me, she confided, "I made my child cry today."

Naturally, I could only assume that, while carrying a loaded laundry basket up steep stairs, she'd toppled a toddler caught in her blind spot or she'd accidentally pinched a child's chin while patiently buckling his bike helmet.

"What happened?" I asked, secretly hoping it was worse than I imagined.

That's when Tina described the series of aggravating child behaviors that had precipitated her coming emotionally unglued. Undone, Supermom had yelled at her offspring in a way that had surprised, saddened, and frightened one of them to tears. (She didn't actually say "surprised." I just made that up in my head.)

My heart started to beat just a little faster while I digested the gruesome tale.

Tina then proceeded to strap all three children into their respective belts and car seats and drove them to her husband's place of employment. Once there, she hopped out of the vehicle and went inside. Since he's a doctor, with a full load of patients, I don't believe she'd thought the entire plan through. The story ends when her husband listens empathetically, hugs her, and sends her back to her vehicle.

Looking concerned, wrapped in a damp beach towel, I nodded along sympathetically. But I'm not going to lie; by the time I was visualizing her idling van in the lot of her husband's clinic, I was practically euphoric.

"That is FANTASTIC!" I bellowed.

My friend's confused look told me that my inappropriate outburst required some explanation.

Like a machine gun, I quickly fired, "No, no, not the yelling. That's too bad. It's not like I'm a fiendish monster. On most days, anyway. I'm totally sorry for your kiddo. Hope he's okay now.

Hope you two were able to work it out. It's not that. Of course not. Yuck, right? It's entirely unfortunate . . .'"

Her countenance gave no indication that my babbling was the least bit comprehensible.

"It's about *me*," I finally confessed. Then, in a lower voice, I admitted, "I thought I was the only one. I thought you were perfect."

Chatting poolside in the sweltering sun, I suddenly felt refreshed and alive. Tina's honesty gave me the energy to drive home, make dinner, give baths, read the single story, and kiss the tops of little heads before bedtime.

As my van pulled out of the gravely pool driveway, I smiled to myself. Because I *wasn't* alone any longer.

I honestly don't know if Tina meant to be transparent or whether authenticity just leaked out because she was at the end of her rope. I *am* convinced that, as we *choose* it, we're set free.

Getting Real

My friend Jennifer Grant tells the story of a friend, Mark, who's a college theater professor. In a clowning exercise that Mark assigns, students must identify a character trait they dislike about themselves and then exaggerate it. Really ham it up.

In a three-minute performance, students play up their oversized flaw—whether it's being extremely shy, or drinking too much, or keeping a messy home—all while wearing a red clown nose. The assignment is meant to free students from being bound by their inhibitions.

Jennifer explains, "They no longer fear others' judgment or being found out. They find strength in their weaknesses."

Now that's freedom.

Grip Released

In describing the way in which, as a pastor, John Lynch aims to live mask-free, he recalled standing in front of his congregation and saying, "I don't pray and read Scripture as much as you think I should."

A stranglehold of shame gave up its grip on me when I heard John had lowered his mask, first to his congregation and then to us. As a clergy person myself, I've never wanted to believe that I'm the only one who doesn't pray and engage Scripture as I ought. This is, in the biz, the sacred cow. I could tell folks among whom I minister that I overeat, that I'm suffering from depression, that I don't read regularly with my kid who needs help reading, or any number of other sordid weaknesses and transgressions. But showing or admitting a lack of consistent devotion to prayer and the reading of Scripture is something I conveniently forget to place on the list of vulnerable confessions. And if I do, I couch it with easily misunderstood disclaimers like "not as often as I'd like" or "not the way I used to."

So to imagine John standing in front of his congregation and being authentic before them—even though he's the pastor!—was absolutely fantastic.

Getting Real

Having received John's wonderful gift and Supermom Tina's wonderful gift, I was empowered to be more authentic myself. I'm really convinced that this is how it works. When we see someone else being who they really are, we're set free to be who we really are. And since I *am* one hot mess, there is plenty of opportunity for being . . . real. Daring to take the first baby steps to freedom, I have begun to let people know how I really am. Let me catch you up to speed.

After ninety minutes of dental work, with the sounds of my favorite music on Pandora, a friendly hygienist, a conscientious dentist who narrates the procedures and tells jokes to relax me, the sound of a drill, and the sound of the suckee thing, I am shaking and ready to burst into tears. It has to do with the way I'm wired. And because I know that many others are able to tolerate this routine so much better than I do, I feel shameful.

I don't go to parties with my husband because the cacophony of conversations leaves me absolutely wrecked. At my kids' elementary school, I've effectively avoided every school picnic and work day for the last three years because, again, the combination of people and sounds overwhelms me. When I'm at my mom's, I pretend to have work to do that prevents me from crossing the hall to have appetizers and dinner with neighbors because I will come home drained. And though this wiring is out of my control, I feel ashamed about who I am and how I am.

> When we see someone else being who they really are, we're set free to be who we really are.

Once a month I plummet into a pit of emotional despair. Though for the last five or six years daily mood-altering medication has helped me remain emotionally stable, lately it has failed to be effective at a predictable point in my monthly cycle. During the day or two that this happens, I experience an excruciating amount of emotional agony. And though I understand that it is a legitimate medical condition I certainly did not order, it still feels shameful.

This is just the preamble to the short list of my character deficits. Anyone in my household could give you a much longer and more extensive listing.

What If It Were Worse?

But what if I'd added more scandalous bits to my list? Assuming you have any heart at all, you'll be gracious and forgiving about my cycle and my sadness and my aural processing troubles. What if I'd confessed to something less forgivable? That I killed my great-aunt with my bare hands or intentionally poisoned my dog? What then?

Lewis Smedes confirms, "To be accepted whether or not we deserve to be accepted has always been an outrage to careful and rigid moralists."[1]

For what it's worth, I don't think you even have to be a careful rigid moralist to take issue with God's unconditional acceptance that receives adulterers and tax collectors and prostitutes and all manner of dirty and shameful sinners. It *is* scandalous! It offends the sensibilities of all of us who work so dang hard to mask up. If *we* have to do it—and of course, in our deep places we believe we do—then *everyone* should have to do it! If everyone starts presenting to others as we really are, bedlam will ensue! But if we can just get gay people to stay in the closet, and alcoholics to sober up for church, and raging mothers to smile in the school carpool lane, then we have some chance of keeping our own anxieties at bay.

Whoop . . . there it is.

When people start living mask-less, who knows what might happen?

When you begin to live real, you give others the gift to do the same. Are you willing to accept, once and for all, that you are, forever, dearly loved and cherished? Can you fathom the possibility that anything you could possibly fear in this life or the next is overwhelmingly conquered by the reality of your eternal belovedness? Will you risk believing that who you are is acceptable to God? Sit with the possibility that God is infinitely more gracious than you have yet dared to believe. Soak in the reality that there is nothing you can do to change God's relentless, passionate love for you.

10

Be Who You *Are*

During the month we were moving between homes, my daughter was sprawled out on the living room floor watching TV. My husband, exhausted from manic packing, was flopped into the single comfortable chair left in the room. As I joined them, the insult of getting the remaining stinky chair stung less—and I also realized the extent of my husband's exhaustion from the manic packing—when I noticed they were watching TLC's hit show *What Not to Wear*. I did not plan to stay long.

I have had all sorts of ideological and personal problems ever since my sister-in-law breathed the fateful sentence years ago: "There's a new reality show on TLC that I think you'd be perfect for!"

Truly, she said it with a smile.

Should you be unfamiliar, the formula for the hit show goes something like this:

1. Friend or family member turns in the name of an offensive dresser in his or her life.
2. Over weeks or days, TLC shoots hidden camera footage, in private and in public, of the victim sporting her hideous wardrobe.

3. Said victim is lured into the studio under false pretense.

4. Stacy and Clinton, the hosts, humiliate and malign the woman whose wardrobe does not measure up, on network television, before millions of viewers.

5. In the end, after some degree of protest, the woman agrees that she is worthy of humiliation, repents, and finally begins dressing fashionably.

So the whole enterprise *depends* on the power of shame. That my daughter excitedly reported that this was the world's first LIVE episode of *What Not to Wear* convinced me to sit around awhile. Because it was the world's first.

The Victim

On this particular episode, two friends—and I use the word very loosely—had turned in Amy for being an atrocious dresser. In the compelling B-roll back story, shot before Amy gets punked, these friends explained that she'd not sustained a romantic relationship past the second date. This, they theorized, was because her bad clothes attracted bad guys. The hope was that with *better clothes* she'd attract the "right" kind of guy.

The audience's cruelty, of course, is a personification of the lying voice with which we all live: *You may dare to think you're acceptable, but you're really not.*

Then the studio audience, and those of us at home lumping on our marginally comfy furniture, were shown the hidden camera footage of real-world Amy in her horribly tacky clothes. We had to look at her shiny-fabric-clad butt bent over the trunk of her car, as well as a host of other horrendous outfits that included, but were not limited to, a huge puffy feather vest and skin-tight neon dresses. They really were bad. And if *I* know they're bad, they're pretty bad.

Like an ax murderer watching a bread thief get executed in the public square, I can't help imagining what the cameras would see if they caught me. I was wearing a Kermit-green shirt, a black cotton skirt over yoga pants cut off at the knee, lime green and white rugby-stripe socks, and daisy-painted combat boots. I also wore fabulous green glasses and delicious lime beads. Though I obviously looked awesome, I could see how these fashion devils could, potentially, turn the bloodthirsty *Hunger Games* audience against me.

And this audience was *vicious*. I've been in the audience of late night talk show filmings, and so I know they have a fun comedian get everyone pumped up and laughing before the host comes out. I think on *What Not to Wear* they must surely hire someone mean who shames people in the audience before the show so that they're feeling like crap and are ready to shame the next poor girl in tacky clothes who walks onstage.

The audience's cruelty, of course, is a personification of the lying voice with which we all live: *You may dare to think you're acceptable, but you're really not.*

As I watch Amy's wardrobe being wheeled out for examination by the vicious hosts, I can't help but picture mine. I see my delicious dyed denim jackets. I see turquoise jeans with paisley fabric sewn to the bottoms. I see T-shirt dresses trimmed in polka-dot ribbon, and glasses and hair clips decorated with cheerful polka dots. The audience in my mind skewers me. One says it looks like a clown wardrobe. Another says I dress like a toddler. Someone piggybacks to say it's not feminine, sexy, or mature. The clear message is that I am *not* acceptable.

I know how it will go for Amy because in the end the victim, wearing a pricy new outfit and new haircut and new makeup, always says, "You were right! I never would have chosen this for myself, but I look great and I feel great! Thank you!" No one has ever, publicly, demanded the return of their puffy feather vest.

In my private musings, as we watch the show, I vow never to say those words. I refuse to say, "You were right." I vow to go to my grave resisting. They could offer me millions to agree, and I'd never concede.

This is how it goes in my head.

During a commercial I let Zoe and Peter in on the drama I've concocted in my mind. As I describe seeing my rainbow wardrobe hung for slaughter—the boots and the jackets and the socks with little antique cars on them—I can hear how it might sound like there could be a grain of truth in whatever it is that Stacy and Clinton might say about it.

To clarify, I announce, "I'm not saying they would be right."

Curious, provocative, Peter clarifies, "So they *wouldn't* be right?"

With a bit of childlike petulance, I retort, "I didn't say that they weren't right. But I still wouldn't give in."

As my husband has come to know, I believe, with vehemence, that even if I'm not accepted, I'm still *acceptable*.

A useful life skill on so many levels.

And though my own beleaguered insistence may very well spring from some unmet developmental need, or some narcissistic demand for attention, the outcome—choosing to silence messages that insist on my inherent unacceptability—really is the singular path to freedom from shame.

In every moment we have the opportunity to *agree* or *disagree* with the insinuation that we're not really acceptable the way we are.

Choosing the Face That Is True

In 1992, just after I'd finished college, I found both of my birthparents for the first time. My birthmother, having herself registered to be reunited two years earlier, was thrilled to know me. My birthfather, who had agreed to a closed adoption twenty-two years earlier, and had *not* registered to be reunited, was less enthusiastic to know me.

When I looked toward the delighted countenance of my birthmother, even before I ever laid eyes on her in person, it glowed, and told me, "I have always held you in my heart and I am so glad to know you. You were perfect then and I think you're pretty spectacular now. I rejoice in you."

When I looked toward my birthfather, though I would *never* literally see him, his purposeful absence expressed, "I thought I'd put all this business with you behind me. I've got other things going right now. I don't think it's going to work out between us."

There I am at a fork in the road, with the opportunity to warm in the glow of her unbridled love for me or to stand waiting, chilled, outside the door of his affection. Without ever making a conscious choice, I heeded his rejecting countenance and rationalized away the gracious acceptance of hers. Of his, my deep insides reasoned, *Yup, this seems about right. This is how it is with me. This is what I deserve.* Of hers, my insides protested, *She doesn't know. If she'd had to live with me, she'd know better. She'd know I'm not really worth sticking around for or loving.* Though never once did I consciously think any of these devilish thoughts—which might have then been subject to reason—they reverberated in the deep circuits of my being.

In every moment we have the opportunity to *agree* or *disagree* with the insinuation that we're not really acceptable the way we are.

As if he had actually found long lost birthparents as he was graduating from college and coming into his own as a young adult, Henri Nouwen identified this naughty logic at work inside me:

> You keep listening to those who seem to reject you. But they never speak about you. They speak about their own limitations. They confess their poverty in the face of your needs and desires. They simply ask for your compassion. They do not say that you are bad, ugly, or despicable. They say only that you are asking for something they cannot give. . . . The sadness is that you perceive their necessary withdrawal as a rejection of you instead of as a call to return home and discover your true belovedness.[1]

Will we continue to tip our faces toward the one turned away from us or will we, instead, return home to discover our true belovedness?

Two Faces

Graciously, there is one who's forged the path ahead of us.

There was this meaningful moment in Jesus's life when he too stood between two paternal authorities. And, like me, the one that first formed him naturally had more traction than the subsequent countenance he faced.

The first father would come to him, though not for the first time, in a desert, and the second, a father of lies, on a mountain.

Jesus's cousin John was out in the desert preaching a new kingdom and baptizing those who confessed their sins and wanted to change. The defining face, though, wasn't John's. It was the beautiful, gracious face of Jesus's Father, announcing, "This is my Son, chosen and marked by my love, delight of my life" (Matt. 3:17 Message).

The Face that is true says to Jesus:

1. You are mine.
2. I chose you.
3. You're marked, branded, identified by my love.
4. I delight in you.

Knowing that Jesus was formed by this face, before his baptism and during it and after it, really explains so very much.

It was the light of that face that gave him the chutzpah to reject the face that lied.

Virtual Parents

With my prayerful imagination, I release my own real birthparents. In their place, I imagine two others, both men. Closing my eyes, I see, with the eyes of my heart, these two different fathers. Standing in the middle of a tree-lined residential street, the real one on which I grew up, there is a home on each side. From the outside, the brick Tudor homes decorated with climbing ivy look identical to my childhood one. Standing in the threshold of each is a father, though neither is the flesh and blood father with whom I was actually raised. Their types, though, are eerily familiar.

On the left, one stands behind a glass storm door. Intuitively, I know that no one else is in there with him. Were he to speak, his voice would be muffled by it. But he is silent. His wide stance and crossed arms communicate clearly that no one will be crossing the threshold of the house. Clenched jaw, furrowed brow, and tense muscles all indicate that he is displeased with whatever hapless soul has caused him to rise and move toward the door in the first place. I fear it's me, that I, somehow, am the object of his wrath. Terrified, I stand frozen in my tracks, willing myself to disappear. I lower my eyes, afraid to meet his disapproving gaze. As if not seeing me at all, he slams the inner wooden door shut and disappears from view.

Turning to the house on the right, I see another father standing out on the porch, animated and expectant, as if he's waiting for someone's return. Music and laughter drift out through the screen door behind him. Sweet, steamy smoke from a grill rises from behind the house, where others seem to be having a party. Expectant for *someone's* arrival, he's shifting his weight back and forth, in time with the tune of Stevie Wonder's *Isn't She Lovely*, which drifts from the house.

His eyes raise, as if he's just seen someone he recognizes, and his face breaks out in a broad smile. As if he just found out he won the lottery, he pumps both fists in the air and skips down the stairs. Picking up speed, he runs down the walkway, over the sidewalk, and is bounding into the street. As he throws his arms wide open, I realize he is coming for *me*. There's no one else. He has recognized me as someone he knows intimately and loves unconditionally. With that confidence, I melt into his warm hug.

Though neither figure is one I've experienced in the flesh, they are both mine. I'm becoming more and more convinced that the one who holds my attention is up to me.

The Face That Is True

To choose God, to agree with God's reality, would be to entertain the weird, unlikely possibility of the guy bounding off his front porch to welcome me into his home-the-way-home-is-supposed-to-be. It's to hear him say, "Margot, I'm delighted to see you, baby. I'm so glad you're here. You know you're my girl, right?"

> **I'm becoming more and more convinced that the one who holds my attention is up to me.**

"*Woman*," I'd correct him, the way I'd chide my mom for using the wrong word. But secretly I'd feel all warm and fuzzy inside.

"That too," he'd quickly concede. "I'm not stuck with you, because I'm bound, by my nature, to love. I know you fear that, but I really want to be with you. And I want for you to experience that it's my love that *defines* you: beloved is who you *are*."

I toy with the possibility: "*Beloved* is *who I am*."

When I see it in the face of the exuberant father, it feels true.

Author Anne Lamott hears Jesus bearing witness to this very thing in the Gospels:

> "Behold the lilies of the field, how they grow; they neither toil nor spin, and yet I tell you, even Solomon in all his glory was not arrayed like one of these." But that's only the minor chord. The major one follows in his anti-anxiety discourse—which is the soul of this passage—that all striving after greater beauty and importance, and greater greatness, is foolishness.[2]

And I would push further to say that striving to please others, in the attempt to make yourself acceptable to them, is also foolishness.

Lamott continues, underscoring your inherent good-enough-ness, confirming, "It is ultimately like trying to catch the wind.

Lilies do not need to do anything to make themselves more glorious or cherished."[3]

You're the lily. I'm the lily. The gospel of gracious good news has
announced that there's nothing we need to do, nothing we can do,
to become what we already are: glorious and cherished.

Margot describes two fathers standing in two doorways. Whether you
imagine fathers or mothers, can you picture these two "types"? Which
one feels more familiar to you? Read about Jesus's telling of the gracious
father in Luke 15:11–32. Allow yourself to stand in the raggedy shoes of
the beloved son. Experience God's gracious embrace of unconditional love.

We Give God a Face

Aware or unaware, many of us have assigned *to God* the expressions we've gleaned from other faces. Some of these match what we know to be true of the Father of Jesus. Many, however—filled with disappointment or heartless judgment—bear no resemblance to the One whose gracious, steadfast love never fails. As we begin to notice these misleading façades, we can at last exchange the false for the true.

11

An Infinite Number of Elrods

Once again, eighty-six-year-old Clara had gotten it into her head that her hallmate Elizabeth, on the dementia wing of a local care facility where I worked, was her dead husband, Elrod. Because I didn't understand exactly how dementia worked, I wasn't clear on exactly what Clara was experiencing. It seemed as though, when she looked at Elizabeth, she actually *saw* Elrod.

Having mounted the stairs from the first floor to the second, punching in the security code to gain access, I entered the unit to find a desperate Elizabeth frantically wheeling her chair down a long hallway to escape Clara. Clara, dressed in a dusty-blue polyester pantsuit, was in pursuit.

Though Elizabeth always wore dresses and ponytails, I would still squint and try to imagine how Elrod must have once appeared. Perhaps he had a head full of white hair, like Elizabeth's. Or maybe he also wore small wiry glasses. He may have had a long, thin face. And though Elizabeth, visibly upset by Clara's constant confusion, insisted she was not Elrod, Clara could not be convinced.

"Elrod!" Clara hollered as I drew closer to the commotion. "You get back here!"

As the fast-wheeling Elizabeth widened the gap between them, Clara shouted even louder, "Don't pretend you don't hear me, Elrod! You get back here this minute!" The spectacle had drawn the attention of the other residents who'd been lingering or chatting in the hallway. All the glaucoma-afflicted and macular-degenerating eyes were glued to the show.

In the training I'd been given, we had learned to not attempt to talk a person experiencing dementia back into the reality everyone else was experiencing. So though I felt no need to remind Clara that Elrod was no longer with us, I did feel obliged to help Elizabeth.

"Clara," I said gently, "I think Elizabeth is trying to go back to her room. Why don't we let her go to her room?"

My interference served only to further enrage Clara. I may as well have told her that Elrod was a slice of cheddar cheese. Had I not been confident that I could outrun her in a footrace, her icy stare would have terrified me.

Impatient, Clara turned abruptly back to Elizabeth. And because I seemed to be coming between them, Clara insisted that Elizabeth, as Elrod, declare his/her loyalties.

"Well," she demanded, "are you coming with *me*, Elrod?"

Everyone in the hallway except Clara knew the answer to that one. Her fiery gaze burned in my direction.

"Or," she hissed at Elizabeth with disgust, gesturing toward me, "are you staying here with . . . the *CREATURE!*"

With all the venom she could muster, she actually called me "the creature." When Elizabeth chose me, Clara wheeled around, furious, and stormed back to her room.

Being identified like some common Scooby Doo villain had left me almost as traumatized as Elizabeth. Though Clara and I were *both* looking at Elizabeth's face, we each saw someone different. There was a real person behind Elizabeth's glasses, but she could not be known unless the mask Clara had superimposed upon her was removed.

America's Four Gods

Even though the majority of us don't suffer from dementia, don't we, in some ways, do the same thing that Clara did to Elizabeth? We impose a face we know onto the face of another.

When Americans "look" at God, we're not all seeing the same Elrod. And though it's no secret that most individuals in the United States "believe in God,"[1] a groundbreaking study from the Baylor Institute for Studies of Religion dug a little bit deeper by asking questions about just who it was that people were seeing. Among nearly four hundred questions about religion, the Baylor Religion Survey included twenty-nine questions about God's character and behavior. Specifically, this research, conducted by the Gallup Organization during the last quarter of 2005, revealed that Americans are far from being of one mind about the *nature* of the God in whom we claim to believe.

I was particularly intrigued to discover how we *see* God. And while most folks in their right mind aren't prepared to reveal to either me or the Baylor researchers that God has a thin, pale face, or white hair, or wiry glasses, the Baylor Religion Survey actually did begin, in a very peripheral way, to describe both the type of face, and the proximity of that face, that people have assigned to God. Even respondents who wouldn't describe God in anthropomorphic language would necessarily describe characteristics that could be assigned human features. For instance, those who identify God as "generous" might visualize a face with warm, gracious eyes. Those who describe God as being "present" might imagine God as an effective listener, with ears that pay attention. Or someone who believed God to be "distant" might visualize a face that was tipped away from her own.

And while Baylor's study makes no reference to any of these physical images, the features of a God-face nonetheless begin to take shape in my heart and mind as I review their data. Descriptions of anger or graciousness elicit particular eyes. Shame or encouragement call to mind certain lips. Whether God listens or is deaf to human cries suggests ears.

What was fascinating to discover, as Americans described the ways in which God behaves, was that not one, but *several* faces begin to take shape. Specifically, researchers discovered very divergent thinking in two distinct areas. One was God's level of engagement. This was the extent to which individuals believe that God is directly involved in worldly and personal affairs. The second area that emerged was God's level of anger. This was described as the extent to which individuals believe that God is angered by human sins and tends toward punishing, severe, and wrathful characteristics.[2]

Based on various combinations of these two dimensions—engagement and anger—researchers identified four types of ways that Americans think about God, with one news outlet trumpeting the study as "America's Four Gods."[3]

Type A is the Authoritarian God
Type B is the Benevolent God
Type C is the Critical God
Type D is the Distant God

So while 85 to 90 percent of Americans claim to "believe" in God, four very distinct expressions of God emerged from the study. The report summarizes:

Type A is the Authoritarian God: Individuals who believe in the Authoritarian God tend to think that God is highly involved in their daily lives and world affairs. They tend to believe that God helps them in their decision-making and is also responsible for global events such as economic upturns or tsunamis. They also tend to feel that God is quite angry and is capable of meting out punishment to those who are unfaithful or ungodly.[4]

This is the angry-faced God who is both physically near and somewhat enmeshed with human beings.

Type B is the Benevolent God: Like believers in the Authoritarian God, believers in a Benevolent God tend to think that God is very active in our daily lives. But these individuals are less likely to believe that God is angry and acts in wrathful ways. Instead, the Benevolent God is mainly a force of positive influence in the world and is less willing to condemn or punish individuals.[5]

This is the gracious-faced God who is physically near and also engaged with human beings.

Type C is the Critical God: Believers in a Critical God feel that God really does not interact with the world. Nevertheless, God still observes the world and views the current state of the world unfavorably. These individuals feel that God's displeasure will be felt in another life and that divine justice may not be of this world.[6]

This is the angry-faced God who is physically distant, and disengaged, from human beings.

Type D is the Distant God: Believers in a Distant God think that God is not active in the world and not especially angry either. These individuals tend towards thinking about God as a cosmic force which set the laws of nature in motion. As such, God does not "do" things in the world and does not hold clear opinions about our activities or world events.[7]

This is the gracious-faced God who is physically distant and disengaged from human beings.

I found myself conflicted as I surveyed these sketches because I'd have a hard time ruling any out. A compelling argument could be made, and ample scriptural support cited, for every single one of the four images!

Study demographics revealed fascinating trends.

If you're a woman, you're more likely to believe in an engaged God.

If you're African American, chances are high that you believe in the Authoritarian God.

If you've got a college degree and earn more than $100,000, you're more likely to believe in a Distant God. The way you might also believe in a distant government. (Sassy wisecracks *mine*.)

And here's a fun party trick for the next time you're snowed in at Chicago's O'Hare airport: the region of the United States in which you live is significant in relation to these four types. Researchers report, "Easterners disproportionately tend towards belief in a Critical God. Southerners tend towards an Authoritarian God. Midwesterners tend towards a Benevolent God and West Coasters tend towards belief in a Distant God."[8]

Fascinating, right?

Two Factors

I was particularly intrigued with the two dimensions of God's nature that emerged in the research: engagement and anger. While they seemed entirely random to me at first, they actually each get at something quite essential and fundamentally meaningful about how we relate to *another*.

The first, *God's level of engagement*, describes the proximity and involvement of God with believers. It suggests whether an individual imagines God as an out-of-state absentee landlord or whether God is like the near grandmother, living down the hall in a mother-in-law suite, who puts a savory dinner on the table each night. Engagement, an almost measurable or quantifiable way to talk about God's nearness, describes how near or far, how engaged or disengaged, God is from a believer. Specifically, it names the degree to which God is *with* us.

The second, *God's level of anger*, gets at what I'd call the *quality* of the countenance of the face that is turned toward the believer. And, though presumably less popular since it didn't garner the kind of attention that respondents afforded to *anger*, one might also surmise that some who tip their faces toward God would see not anger or disinterest, but rather a gracious, welcoming countenance. This axis names the degree to which God is *for* us.

Though intended to describe God, these terms could also be employed to represent regular relationships in the regular world.

They could describe relationships with coworkers or neighbors or bank tellers or spouses.

Let's consider, for a moment, the parent-child relationship. The Critical Parent would be the one who, out of the picture, still condemns. Though absent—to military assignment or prison, to death or divorce—the eyes of this one continue to judge. The Authoritarian Parent would also be angry, judgmental, but this one is nearby. It's Tiger Mom, the helicopter parent. The Distant Parent is removed, but gracious. He's the Disney Dad who's mostly absent, but swoops in annually to take his kids on a fun trip. The Benevolent Parent is both near and gracious, a positive influence who's available to the child.

Do any of these sound familiar?

I've got my fingers crossed that Baylor might be planning *another* study for those surveyed to answer the exact same battery of questions about their earliest caregivers. Specifically I'd be interested in the way their answers corresponded to their original survey. Now *that* I'd like to see!

> It's not only our earliest caregivers who give shape to this visage we give to God. It is also formed by the Religious—church members, professional clergy, and others—who come to represent God.

Formative Influences

It's not only our earliest caregivers who give shape to this visage we give to God. It is also formed by the Religious—church members, professional clergy, and others—who come to represent God. In his recent memoir, *All Is Grace*, Brennan Manning identifies two of the people who influenced his internal blueprint for God as his mother and his childhood priest. Had Manning participated in Baylor's study, his description would most certainly have matched Critical God.

Manning, raised Roman Catholic and later ordained as a priest himself, explains, "In addition to believing God was 'something awful,' I also experienced Him as 'separate.'"⁹ He unwittingly—or perhaps quite wittingly—names the two axes charting God's *for*-ness and *with*-ness. In order to give flesh to these, Manning describes a typical childhood experience in the confessional booth:

> Most of the time I swear it seemed like the priest was angry. He was often almost screaming, something like this:
>
> Priest: Don't you have any respect for your parents? How dare you disobey them! Tell me exactly what you did and do not leave anything out!
>
> Me: My mother sent me to the store to buy a pound of lean bacon and I forgot and bought a pound of fatty. My mother got angry because I disobeyed.[10]

Manning explains,

> Through the voices of those angry priests, I heard an awful, angry God separate from me and my life. So, like I did at home, I vowed to do what was required for me to avoid punishment: I tried my best to be a good Catholic boy. I even mustered up the courage and tried out one year to be an altar boy, but for some reason I couldn't memorize the Latin. I knew that I had disappointed the priest (he told me as much), which meant I obviously had disappointed God (why would God disagree with the priest?), and that reinforced my mother's words about me (which she'd stated more than once): *He'll never amount to much*.[11]

None of us have received, in perfect human form, the love for which we were made.

An unholy trifecta, to be sure.

Children naturally believe that they deserve what they get. If a parent is physically or emotionally distant, the child believes she is not worthy of sustained presence. If a parent is critical or furious or disappointed, the child believes that he is not worthy of a gracious one.

And the rub, of course, which is so poignantly illustrated by Manning's experience: *none of us* have experienced human parents who were constantly present and unfailingly gracious. You haven't. I haven't. The three children who live under my roof most certainly haven't. None of us have received, in perfect human form, the love for which we were made.

Less-Than-Perfect Parents

If you could hear the tone of my voice saying these words out loud, I believe your ear would register them as being malice-free: "Every one of my caregivers did the best they could do. But because of their human nature—unable to be constantly present and perfectly gracious—there were gaps in my experience of being loved." Though I purpose to love my children in the best way I know how, I am *inherently unable* to be constantly present and perfectly gracious.

Not possible.

For example, each springtime my children all play sports for various leagues throughout our city. Zoe plays in an all-girls soccer league. Rollie and Abhi play in coed leagues. Some years the boys have been on separate teams, and other years they've played on the same team. Invariably, there will be a Saturday morning in which all three children have simultaneous games on various fields spread throughout the city. Without fail, these weeks with overlapping game times usually coincide with a weekend where either I or my husband is traveling out of town. Of course. We have a great support network, friends and family, who help us get each child to the right place at something that approximates the right time. But, limited by time and space, Peter and I have been unable to be present to each child in every moment. We were *for* them, but we weren't always *with* them.

The converse, although far less benign, is equally true. When we are *with* our children, we are not always *for* them as they want us and need us to be. Though I'd say we're the sort of parents who are, on the whole, *mostly* good enough, we fail all the time. We become impatient. We practice selfishness. We rage. We shame. We are not consistently *for* our children in the ways they want and need us to be.

Whatever God-image of otherness they glean from us will be *necessarily* imperfect.

And to top it all off, each child comes into the world wired with her or his own unique sensitivities that impact their perceptions. For example, one might have enough happy dopamine pulsing through her veins so that our worst failures will roll off her back like water, while another is naturally more sensitive. Which means it's entirely possible that the "blueprint" that has been the parental offering of my husband and I, the one that has necessarily been laid in each little heart, could be read *differently* in the heart of each of our children. In fact, I'm certain of it. So while one might have the internal resources to tolerate a higher degree of failure on our parts without concluding that our failure implies his unworthiness, another, more sensitive and inherently less resourced, might easily *equate* our failings with her inherent worthiness of love.

The complicated formula particular to every individual adds up to one thing: an imprint of "other" that is seared into the heart of each person. That deep, incalculable pattern—what we expect of an "other"—will quietly influence who we befriend, who we might marry, and even how we see God.

So while the folks at Baylor identified what some have called "America's Four Gods," I suspect there are—most certainly—more. Not an infinite number, but a finite one. The number is equal to the number of individuals who have ever lived who have, consciously or unconsciously, given a face to God.

Researchers at Baylor identified four "types" of God: Authoritarian, Benevolent, Critical, and Distant. Which one of these images most immediately resonates with you? To what degree do you sense that God is **with** you? To what degree do you think that God is **for** you? As you pause to reflect, does the image you hold match what you know to be revealed about God in the Scriptures? Does it match the face of Jesus?

12

My Mom's Face
on Jesus's Body

Erin had been raised in the Roman Catholic Church. When she was young, Erin had nightmares frequently. She describes the relief she found during difficult nights. Erin explains, "It was only by imagining Mary or God with the head of my mother imposed on her/his body that I was able to get through the night. Since my mother was the most Christ-like of anyone I knew, and my earliest example of him, it was easiest to imagine God as a benevolent parent who loved unconditionally and worked all things for good."

Though it so often goes awry, what with sin and shame and all, I have to believe that Erin's natural projection of a caregiver's countenance, as a source of real comfort, was stitched into God's good design and intention for human beings.

Keenly aware that her mother's face and voice and body have allowed her to know a God who is good, today Erin riffs:

God smells like powder. God changes the oil, likes to get his hands dirty. God is a champion hula-hooper. God drives a church bus.

God gives rides to strangers, finds furniture for single moms, and speaks comfort in prisons. God is not legalistic, likes to do things her own way. God is whimsical like the wind. God handles snakes, mice, and hermit crabs without gagging. God is sensitive but can't be manipulated. God loves to dance, ballroom or booty. And God sings along to The Chiffons on the oldies stations.

Frank Lake explains, "Faith, on the basis of past good experiences still reverberating on the circuits of memory, gives 'body' or reliable 'substance' to the one who is longed-for."[1] When Erin lay in bed as a child, feeling fear, the good experience of a reliable other continued to reverberate on the circuits of her memory, giving reliable substance to the one she longed for when she could not see God.

Like Erin, each of us holds a deep memory, as if in our bones, of whether or not a gracious person is with us and for us. James Loder elaborates on the early interaction between child and parent. "In the face-to-face interaction (whether actualized or remaining an innate potential), the child seeks a *cosmic-ordering, self-confirming impact from the presence of a loving other*."[2] What he's saying with the big words is that every kid is seeking, in the face of his or her caregiver, the presence of a loving person, human or divine, who orders their world and their identity.

In the face-to-face interaction with a caregiver, the child is after two things: he seeks presence, the assurance that someone reliable is *with* him, and he seeks graciousness, the assurance that someone reliable is *for* him. As it was with Erin, sometimes the face toward which we turn is indeed gracious. Other times, however, the human face toward which we turn fails to reflect to us the face of God.

The Face of a Busy God

Krista is thirty-four. A committed Christian, she explains, "My dad was always a strong, steady provider for our family. He's wise. He's understanding. I feel safe with him."

If this God-is-like-Dad business is true, you'd think that Krista would be set, right? She even describes her dad as a good listener.

Krista continues to explain, "But my dad worked a lot. He'd hole himself up in the office and I never wanted to bother him unless it was a really big deal. It needed to be a very good reason. I tried very hard to be low-maintenance and not go to him unless I was in a real pickle." And because Krista was brave and competent, the arrangement worked out.

What Krista learned from an early age, from a workaholic father and a mother who was easily upset, was *independence*. Self-sufficiency. She chose to handle hardship privately, rather than to share it with either of them so as not to add to what they already had on their plates—for her dad, work, and for her mom, worry.

> Each of us holds a deep memory, as if in our bones, of whether or not a gracious person is with us and for us.

As is so often the case, Krista married a man a lot like her dad. And over the first nine years of their marriage, this very issue had been a sticking point for them. Though he was ready and willing to receive her, Krista never wanted to trouble her husband, fearing she'd add to his stress. She didn't want to be a burden.

There's one more person whose face matches the one Krista saw on her dad and eventually her husband. Krista had also assigned to *God* the same face.

Krista explains, "I never envisioned God making eye contact with me. He was in the office and I knocked lightly at the door. 'Um, God . . . do you have a sec? I just want to ask you one thing really quick . . .'" A voice in her head would concur, *See, he's really busy. Just handle it on your own.*

In her right mind, Krista was aware of what she did. She understood, at some level, that an overscheduled, hard-to-access father was *not* the Father of Jesus. In her most lucid moments, Krista realized that she'd been prone to live independently from God because she'd accepted something about God—namely, God's remoteness and disinterest—that was not true.

Last fall, Krista attended a spiritual retreat where she was invited to notice, with God's help, any agreements she'd made about God's character that weren't true. This thing about being a bothersome burden was what God so graciously revealed to Krista. Krista now explains, with excitement in her voice, "I heard God say that he was *here* for me. He was pursuing me and wanting my time and hoping I would come to him always, every moment of every day. He is *eager* to spend time with me. And it doesn't have to be a big reason. Any ol' reason will do."

And when asked about God's face and voice, she now beams. "I think God smiles when we talk, definitely. He has raised, interested eyebrows. He has a soft tone of voice."

Willing to recognize her distorted image of God, Krista was able to replace it with the face that is true.

Krista had naturally projected onto God very human characteristics she'd gleaned from her father. She had anticipated that God would engage with her the way her human father did. She'd accepted the calculation so many of us agree to:

Present, available, receiving caregiver = present, available, receiving God

Absent, unavailable, rejecting caregiver = absent, unavailable, rejecting God

Despite my initial dogged resistance to the idea, I've become convinced that our insides are naturally patterned to anticipate and recognize a holy God who is like our earliest and most influential human caregivers.

True and False, Conscious and Subconscious

While Erin's transference of familiar human attributes to God was *conscious*, Krista's was, for years—as most of ours are—

subconscious. In fact, because the faces we give to God often remain unexamined, many "Christians" will go to the grave assuming, either consciously or unconsciously, God is disappointed, angry, frustrated, cruel, or disinterested. It brings a little smile to my face to imagine the eye-opening experience these ones will have the moment they—we!—encounter the God who is real. The way it goes in my mind is that the mask they've given to God—disappointed, angry, frustrated, cruel, or disinterested—is simply dashed, immediately forgotten, by the shine of God's true face.

My friend Hank shares, "My mother was unpredictable and capricious. She'd turn on me the moment I was happy." Though his mother had good moments, she wasn't able to be consistently present to Hank. He continues, "In my late twenties I realized I had an expectation that God would do the same—that I might turn to God only to have God reject me. I expected God to abandon me too." Hank's subconscious understanding of God eventually surfaced to awareness.

If Lake's claim that past *good* experiences give substance to the God who is true, then its converse, in Hank's experience and others, is equally true: bad experiences, still reverberating on the circuits of memory, suggest the *absence* of God. Lake confirms, "The infant spirit looks out fearfully towards a 'god' whose face is full of scorn at its own, evidently contemptible, face."[3] What the infant perceives and swallows whole from the unavailable or ungracious mother is a sense of worthlessness. Hank had no idea—could have no idea!—from his mother's face that God, a steadfast and reliable presence, would never leave nor forsake him.

Help My Unbelief

I was recently chatting with a friend who loves God deeply. Ed believes passionately in God's unconditional love and unflagging grace for every single individual he encounters. He believes it and he shares it freely with others. To watch Ed interact with folks at his church and workplace and on the street proves his authentic love for the ones he's *convinced* that God loves.

But it is harder for him to believe that God loves *Ed*. Humbly, he confessed, "I believe that God loves others, but am not sure God loves me." Though I do not know all of Ed's story, I wondered if Ed had been found inherently unacceptable by someone of importance at an early age.

> **It is not enough to remain guarded, say a prayer, and hope to be accepted by God.**

As he continued to share, Ed disclosed that, because he had a brother with a cognitive impairment, he always felt as though others viewed his entire family as being "not good enough." Defective. Ed had internalized a cadre of faces that he supposed looked on him with shame. Despite God's insistence that he is worthy, Ed protests, insisting that God can't possibly love what other important eyes have seen as unlovable.

I know, from my own experience, that my friend cannot be free of the internalized shaming gaze until he encounters, in a transforming way, the face that receives us exactly as we are. I hear the presumption in that. It sounds as if I'm suggesting that Ed, whom I know to be much more faithful and intimate with God than I am, is simply lacking some particular *quality* of relationship with the Almighty. It almost sounds as if I'm suggesting that if he tried really hard, and believed just the right Scriptures, and prayed a little more, Ed would at long last experience God's acceptance.

No, of course not.

I do, though, believe that for transformation to happen, we need the courage to be unflinchingly real with ourselves about the lies we've believed. Having acknowledged the discrepancy between his proclamation and what he believes to be true, Ed is most certainly on that journey.

I'm on it too, but it certainly began against my will. Given my druthers, I never would have *chosen* vulnerability. I would have much preferred to stay masked up, leaving my costumed God that way as well. But if we are to encounter God face-to-face, we have to take off the layered masks we wear—even the mask of unwavering faith!—and gaze upon God's true countenance. While I believe that Ed can and has and does see God's gracious face tipped toward others, he must now come naked, unmasked, before the God who is real and who longs to confirm his own worthiness.

The transforming encounter with the One who is real is to welcome God to see every square inch of our real selves and to remain vulnerable to his kindliness and welcome. It is not enough to remain guarded, say a prayer, and hope to be accepted by God. Rather, we need to allow God to look upon all of our wretchedness, our guilt, and our shame, and in turn really see his unchanging and loving gaze.

The Power of Encountering the Holy

Remember my friend Don? God looked and sounded and scolded and shamed Don like his stern grandmother. That wasn't a face or voice that Don had consciously chosen—but it was one that was hard to shake. Being cognizant of it was his first step toward change. Accessing another face to replace it, though, is where Don would eventually be transformed.

During seminary, when students would visit Dr. Loder's office, he would, in a pastoral way, pose an interesting question. He would ask the student if they had experienced any encounters with the Holy. He wasn't asking if they've been dutiful about slogging through quiet times every morning. He wasn't asking if they attended church regularly. Rather, he wanted to know if—even *once* in their lifetime—they'd experienced the palpable loving presence of God. He called these encounters "convictional experiences."

Dr. Loder was aware of the way we tend to dismiss these types of "mountaintop" encounters—whether we experienced a divine healing, or heard God's audible voice, or were personally addressed by God through another—as a *deluded high*, the kind so often experienced on a weekend spiritual retreat. Dr. Loder, though, welcomed and employed any recalled experience of God's personal presence with an individual as the *starting point* for transformation. He identified these encounters as being real, inviting individuals to choose *for*, and live *into*, the reality of God's steadfast faithful presence. "Convictional experiences," Loder claims, "are the fulfillment of . . . hope because they present in manifest terms the presence of God; they become his Face for the believer."[4]

Does that make sense? The place where we've *encountered God*, not just where we've sung about God or read words about God, is the place where we become able to experience a face that is true.

My friend Mary Jo encountered God's living presence, recently, in a vision. She explains, "I was waiting at a gate, looking for him to come. I looked away, and then when I looked back he was there. I ran out to him and he let me hug him with all my might." She continues, "He laughed and said, 'Well, of course I would come!'" Now don't you just want to score an invitation so you can meet that guy too? That gracious "of course I would come" face is one to which Mary Jo can return whenever she is in search of the face that is true. In fact, it is the only face that will satisfy.

Loder teaches that another person can never satisfy the primal longing for a face that will not go away. When that longing is met by a spiritual encounter with Christ—the face of God—we are set free to give and receive love freely. Assured of God's presence, we need not fear abandonment from others. Assured that it is Christ's love, in us and through us, which is loving others, we need not fear unhealthy entanglement with others. When we've encountered the real face of God, glowing with gracious, unconditional acceptance, we're at last free to

> When we've encountered the real face of God, glowing with gracious, unconditional acceptance, we're at last free to live and to love in a way that does not try to make another person the missing face.

live and to love in a way that does not try to make another person the missing face.

I'm not sure if you find this as thrilling as I do, but it is really, *really* good news. I'm absolutely convinced that this is what God is actively about in human hearts. We know we have seen the face that is gracious when we recognize eyes of a holy Love that look upon us—really *seeing* us—and, in spite of what is seen, go on looking in kindliness and welcome.

This beautiful Face is not out of reach.

Ask the Holy Spirit to help you notice any agreements you have made about God's character that are not true. Have you, without ever intending to, believed that God is like the parent who left or ignored or hurt or neglected you? In what ways have you believed that God is other than gracious? Offer these to God and invite God to replace them with truth.

13

Gravy Boat God

When I asked about what image she might have attached to God as a child, my pastor friend Angie confessed, "God looked a lot like Charlton Heston in *The Ten Commandments*: stately, somber, white skin, long white beard."

On the chance that you missed it in theaters, a young Charlton Heston played Moses in the 1956 epic film *The Ten Commandments*. And when he encounters God in a burning bush, the bellowing voice actually sounds like an app you could download to make your voice sound deep and booming and echoing.

You know, like God.

For reasons unknown, possibly the wish of director Cecil B. DeMille, the actor responsible for the voice of God wasn't credited in *The Ten Commandments*. So, for years, there was speculation about who had actually mouthed the words of the Almighty. Many guessed it to be the director himself.

In a 1999 interview, over forty years after the making of the film, DeMille's Moses cleared up the mystery.

While they were still in Egypt, Heston explained, filming at Mount Sinai, the cast stayed at the monastery of St. Catherine's.

As they were sharing dinner one evening with the chief abbot of the monastery and DeMille, the conversation turned to who would perform the voice of God.

Heston said, "I saw an opportunity, and I said, 'You know, Mr. DeMille, it seems to me that any man hears the voice of God from inside himself. And I would like to be the voice of God.'"

In the modern vernacular of the Hebrew Bible, people, we call that *chutzpah*.

DeMille was not convinced, hedging, "Well, you know, Chuck, you've got a pretty good part as it is."

That's when the abbot chimed in. "That's an interesting idea though."

Heston, who in fact was eventually granted the honor of voicing God in the burning bush, credited the abbot for tipping the scales in his favor.[1]

Heston's deep bass would be the audible voice that would echo in the hearts and minds of many.

The Ways We "See" God

The same way many of us who haven't heard God audibly have assigned to God a voice like Heston's or the booming voice of our favorite preacher, we've also given God a human face. We naturally carry "pictures" of God in our brains the way proud grandparents carry wallet-size pictures of their grandchildren. And while Hollywood has been more reticent, wisely I think, to *picture* the Almighty, we have still gleaned, from a variety of sources, a number of images that we have—consciously or unconsciously, in whole or in part—assigned to God.

For some of us, the picture is one of a long-bearded, grandfatherly figure like the one Michelangelo painted on the ceiling of the Sistine Chapel. Others see the long-haired, dark-blond, blue-eyed portrait of Jesus that hung in the Sunday school hallway of their grandmother's church. Many admit to envisaging someone who looks like Gandalf from the Lord of the Rings series.

Optimists, believing in a benevolent provider, might see something closer to popular images of the Santa Claus legend. Conversely, unbelievers might conceptualize God as the impotent green glowing head that Dorothy encountered in Oz, no more than the puppet of a fraud.

Identifying the images *we've* assigned to God, both the ones that rush to our minds and the ones we're slower to recognize, isn't nearly as easy and fun as image-googling "Jesus." Fancying ourselves sophisticated, we resist giving physical form to a spiritual being. Those of us who've moved beyond the kind of concrete thinking that attaches a physical representation to that which exists outside of the physical world are less willing to admit, or even recognize, that we might actually visualize God as an older, bearded, deep-voiced white man.

That we're unwilling to admit it makes the fact that we most likely do attach some sort of image to the Almighty no less true. In *How God Changes Your Brain*, Andrew Newberg, MD, and Mark Robert Waldman report that ideas seem to be associated with visual-spatial circuits in the brains of both children *and* adults. "Thus," they explain, "for anyone, the brain's first response is to assign an image to the concept of God."[2]

That our neural networks naturally designate an image we cannot perceive with our senses makes complete sense to me. The same way I cannot see, hear, touch, taste, or smell Napoleon Bonaparte, my brain beelines to an image of an eighteenth-century painting I have stored away in the recesses of my memory when I conceptualize "Napoleon Bonaparte." The same is true of Alexander the Great, Saint Francis of Assisi, and Mother Teresa. I attach a mental image to the person with whom I have no physical access. And though it feels a bit embarrassing to admit it, I do the same with God.

Children, of course, are unabashed about it. When my daughter was three, she had playfully thrown her beloved stuffed puppy Woof-Woof into the backseat of our Camry station wagon. As we drove, she became more and more distressed that her canine was far out of reach of either my long arms glued to the steering wheel or her short ones bound by her car seat. Racking her brain to come up with someone who might possibly be of help, she groaned in despair, "The Lord cannot get my puppy because he's in my heart." For Zoe to imagine God, God needed to physically inhabit—as I'm sure she'd been told in Sunday school—the chest cavity where her pulmonary arteries and veins converged.

And while the long arms of many of us are busy patting ourselves on the back because we no longer actually think a tiny action-figure God has taken up residence in our chest cavity the same way miniaturized genies live in golden gravy boats, many of us have not replaced the fallacy with a more suitable image. So while it's meaningful that we've learned to think abstractly about God as love or light or Spirit, those of us who claim to relate to God aren't in relationship with a red heart symbol or a light bulb or a steamy vapor.

We're in relationship with a personal being.

Personal Images of God

When I asked some friends how they "pictured" God, one referenced the iconic long-bearded wizard of *Harry Potter* fame. She confessed, "I struggle with banishing the Albus Dumbledore look-alike (male, long white hair with a beard) that I unfortunately think children take away from their childhood experiences. He occasionally still shows up."

I suspect that her confession is true for many. The very first chapter of the Bible confirms that we've been made in God's image. And though scholars throughout the centuries have made different guesses about just how we reflect this image—through reason, or creativity, or morality—there's no overarching agreement. Though we don't *really* believe God is available today for us to see in human form, we are often, naturally, tempted to revert to those very early images of God that are anthropomorphic. Newberg and Waldman confirm, "When it comes to our most primal sense of God, it all begins with a face."[3]

To assign a human face to God is how we're naturally wired. Waldman and Newberg explain the way young children, who simply aren't yet able to grasp abstract concepts such as peace or democracy, will assign an image to the concept the way they would any other object. They explain, "A young child's brain has no choice but to visualize God as a face that is located somewhere in the seeable physical world."[4] That we do, both consciously and unconsciously, imagine God as bearing a human face is riddled with both promise and pitfalls.

In God's face, we discover something about who God is and how God relates to us.

The promise is that our prayerful imaginations can recognize God's presence when we come across it.

One man, Bradley, who shared his image of God, offered, "Interestingly enough, the image looks a lot like my dad, and a couple of very knowing, caring, empathetic faces on two beautiful young ladies giving their condolences after my brother's death. It is the warmth of being known." For Bradley, the image of a human face—one of which happened to be the face of his white European American male father—connected him to God.

A very similar countenance, though, for others, can be a warped perversion of the face that is true. My friend Sameer, whose parents are from India, grew up Hindu in Idaho. He reports, "It always seemed to me like God was just a huge inflatable white man."

Sameer really has a way with words.

Though most white Americans take it for granted, it's more than a little bit nutty that popular *Far Side* illustrator Gary Larson can dress an old, bearded white man in a dress and sandals, maybe stand him on some clouds, and his audience *knows* that it's God. If you don't find it nutty, you may be in need of some sort of cultural cleansing bath.

After noodling on it a bit, Sameer acknowledged, "I *did* internalize the old-white-man God, because to some extent it is impossible not to when growing up in the US, especially in Nampa,

Idaho." Sameer explains, "But to the extent that I do not resemble the paradigm human person being inflated to come up with that image, I internalized it as an anxiety rather than as a living source of comfort." Sameer's experience is, of course, one that could be claimed by countless others. Popular images of God exclude them in a culturally specific way, evoking anxiety rather than comfort.

Beyond Shape and Color

Age, race, gender, and privilege aren't the only categories that are registered in the images we've seen and have given to God. More importantly, perhaps, the *character* of God registers on the countenance we assign to the Almighty. Whether we see God as the old bearded white man or as someone who walked the earth looking more like Sadam Hussein may matter less than the *expressions* that are formed by the face we encounter.

In God's face, we discover something about who God is and how God relates to us. Waldman and Newberg explain, "If you tell a child that God can see you, or listen to your prayers, then the child's imagination will associate those qualities with the eyes and ears of a face. If you tell that same child that God gets angry, the brain will generate images of frowns, gritted teeth, or perhaps fists banging against a wall—visual constructions that represent how a child perceives anger in other human beings."[5] The face that we've too often uncritically assigned to God reveals more about God than we might expect.

Were you to close your eyes and search for the face of God, how would those features receive you? Would the eyes be delighted or judging? Would the mouth be turned up or hissing shame? Would the ears be tipped to hear what your life is like, or would they be deaf to your voice? Once you're able to give some form to the face you've given to God, you're then able to decide whether or not it matches the face of Jesus's Father as it is revealed in Scripture.

If deleting a no-longer-useful mental sketch of an old, bearded white man were as easy as erasing a pencil sketch from paper, or if scrapping the angry, booming, deep bass voice were as easy as deleting an MP3 file, lots of us might gladly replace our conceptions with an image or a sound more fitting. However, research indicates that the many images of God we've internalized are largely hidden from our consciousness.

If that story sounds familiar, it's because we're often no more conscious of the masks we've assigned to God than we are of the wily internalized ones with which we view and speak to ourselves. When one of our culture's popular images for God resonates with the one held in our hearts—a bearded white guy or a critical, judging parent or an absent, unconcerned one—the costumed God we've created gains more traction still.

Though I've tried to rinse pale, handsome, twentysomething, light-brown-haired Jesus from the recesses of my heart and mind, when I'm honest, he lingers. I could spend a lot of energy beating myself up for my horrible Eurocentric worldview. But what would that accomplish?

However, if he's white because I assume only white folks have power, that's problematic.

Or if he's pale because I assume God has a preference for light skin, that's also problematic.

Those kinds of assumptions *need* to be challenged.

I've come to suspect, though, that whether the face I give to the person of Jesus looks like vanilla Charlton Heston from *The Ten Commandments* or chocolate Morgan Freeman from *Bruce Almighty* or female deity Alanis Morrisette from *Dogma* is less important than whether that face is available and tipped toward me. The hue or contours aren't as critical as the expression I recognize on the face as its eyes meet mine. Baritone or bass or soprano voice matters less than the intention and graciousness of the one who speaks the words.

I won't flog myself for assigning a human face to either the person of Jesus or his heavenly dad. If that fleshy eye-nose-mouth-ear collage sees and hears and speaks with the gracious intention of the God who is *real*, I welcome it.

A Wonderfully Disturbing New Image

Written as a story for his six kids and a few friends, William P. Young originally self-published just fifteen copies of his novel *The Shack*. Before Young's protagonist, Mack, encountered God in tangible form, his friend asked him what he thought God looked like.

Mack answered, "I don't know. Maybe he's a really bright light, or a burning bush. I've always sort of pictured him as a really big grandpa with a long white flowing beard, sort of like Gandalf in Tolkien's *Lord of the Rings*."[6]

Mack's picture of God sounds like one shared by many.

The encounter fictional Mack would eventually have with a God-figure that was decidedly *not* a bearded white man became, for a moment, a hot-button topic in the evangelical Christian community. We could have dealt with Gandalf. But many of us were more ambivalent about the deity Mack encountered.

> If that fleshy eye-nose-mouth-ear collage sees and hears and speaks with the gracious intention of the God who is *real*, I welcome it.

When Mack banged on the door of a shack in the woods, the door was opened by a large, beaming, African American woman. Who was God.

Mack jumped back.

Young writes:

> With speed that belied her size, she crossed the distance between them and engulfed him in her arms, lifting him clear off his feet and spinning him around like a little child. And all the while she was shouting his name—"Mackenzie Allen Phillips"—with the ardor of someone seeing a long-lost and deeply-loved relative. She finally set him back on Earth and, with her hands on his shoulders, pushed him back as if to get a good look at him.[7]

What makes Young's portrayal of the first person of the Trinity controversial, I believe, isn't that Father God was given flesh. It was that *this* flesh, the flesh of a warm, welcoming, effusive black woman, was what Young chose to portray God.

When God notices the warm tears welling up behind Mack's eyes, she comforts him. "It's okay, honey, you can let it all out. . . . I know you've been hurt, and I know you're angry and confused. So, go ahead and let it out. It does a soul good to let the waters run once in a while—the healing waters." Mack struggled to keep his composure. "Meanwhile," Young writes, "this woman stood with her arms outstretched as if they were the very arms of his mother. He felt the presence of love. It was warm, inviting, melting."[8]

Though the biblical witness doesn't mention *all* the details Young included—effusive, dark-skinned, big-boned—he did get a number right: compassion, empathy, attentiveness, kindness, and gentleness.

These Situations

In these types of heartwarming situations, not unlike the ones shared by those who have experienced near-death moments, I like to begin by asking two questions:

1. Does the description resemble what is proclaimed about God in the Bible?
2. Does any part of it contradict what we know to be true of God from the Bible?

If the answer to the first is "no," if God is portrayed as vindictive and petty and cruel, then I'll discard the image as being worthless. If the answer to the second is "yes," I'll also trash the image.

But if the creative image of God I'm poking at passes these first two questions, I'll make it jump through one last hoop.

For the third and final question, I'll bring to mind a different image. I'll try to picture whatever image of God I currently have nestled quietly, unobtrusively, in my mind and ask the following:

3. Is the *new* rendering *more* true or less true than the image I currently hold?

In this particular case, I was forced to judge for myself whether a robust black female who demonstrates concern, warmth, compassion, and kindness more closely approximated the God revealed in the Scriptures than the image I was currently holding.

Guess whose image of God just got a facelift?

I encourage you to keep these questions handy for the next time you see God portrayed on film, in literature, or in the pages of a news magazine. If the image of God resonates with the character of God communicated in Scripture and doesn't contradict it, if the face given to God is more lifelike and authentic than the one you've been using, you may just have gotten a legitimate and healthy glimpse of the Holy One.

What was your earliest "image" of God? Did you glean a visual picture of Jesus or God from a storybook or movie? Do you have an image of God that comes to mind today? Describe it. In what ways does this image *match* the face of God that's rendered in the Bible, especially as it's reflected by Jesus in the Gospels? In what ways does this image *contradict* the picture of God that Jesus reveals? Discarding what is no longer useful, open your heart to welcome a face and voice that authentically reflect the God of love.

We Encounter the Face That Is True

When we encounter the face of Jesus's Father—as it truly is—we see and are seen by a face like no other. Throughout the Scriptures, and uniquely in the Gospel accounts of Jesus, we see this face as it's reflected to people like us. We are even able to recognize holy glimpses of it in human faces that effectively reflect, for us, what God's face is like.

14

Longing to Be Delivered by a Redemptive Face

few weeks ago, hungry to be entertained, my family started watching *Once Upon a Time* on Hulu. I'm blaming them for drawing me in. The characters in the fictional modern-day town of Storybrook—ostensibly a mayor, a reporter, a teacher, and a tow truck driver—are actually fairy tale characters—a wicked queen, a genie, Snow White, and the little mouse who stitched Cinderella's clothes—who have forgotten who they were when they lived in fairytale land.

So it's very believable.

Our favorite guy in the show is Rumplestiltskin, who turns out to be the evil mastermind behind so much mayhem in fairy tale land. There have been some great film and television bad guys, but this guy, played by Robert Carlyle, really is one of the best. Besides spinning gold, this devil offers magic potions to heroes and villains who get themselves in a pinch. He warns each one, with a devilish gleam in his eye and squeaky, sinister cackle, "Magic always comes at a price!" Despite this eerie warning, these iconic characters, itchy to take the bull by the horns, or the princess by the lips, are always too shortsighted to see how the magic potion will not, in the end, serve them well.

It *always* goes bad.

More specifically, the bad outcome is directly related to whatever spell seemed like such a good idea in the first place. Snow White's gulp of magic potion, to forget Prince Charming forever, causes her to forget who she really is and turns her into a nasty old wench. The wish of a gravy-boat genie, to be with Snow White's evil stepmom forever, gets him trapped, for all eternity, in her magic mirror. Magic always comes with a price. The price is that the outcome becomes a function of the naughty magic.

The Pattern of Transformation

What the show calls *magic* is what I'd call *transformation*. And this is, in fact, how transformation goes. Whether sleepy Snow White falls prey to the bad-apple scheme of the evil queen, or whether she's redeemed by the kiss of Prince Charming, the result of the transformation always bears the mark of whoever mediated it.

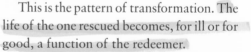

This is the pattern of transformation. The life of the one rescued becomes, for ill or for good, a function of the redeemer.

The longing of the captive heart is that a saving face, with sufficient power to extricate us from our bind, will redeem and transform.

When a princess was chosen by the prince, her "happily ever after" meant that her life became a *function* of his when she became his bride. Snow White. Cinderella. Little Mermaid. (Aka: happily ever after!)

Or today, when a girl, itchy to leave her childhood home, flees with her pimp, her life becomes a function of the one who mediated her release. When a boy, anxious to leave his childhood home, joins a gang, his life becomes a function of that which mediated his release.

This is also the pattern of biblical narratives. Joseph the dreamer. Moses and the Israelites. Jairus's sick daughter. Dying and rising Jesus Christ.

Each is met by the gracious intervention of a powerful mediator, and the continuing effects of the liberation event ripple into the future.

When author C. S. Lewis came to faith in Christ, he had studied all the dying and rising God myths in different cultures and religions. What dawned on him, as he turned his face toward Christ, was that in Jesus the story has come *true*. Here were all these similar stories from different cultures, and in the person of Jesus of Nazareth the story had come true. Here, at last, was the face that truly satisfies.

Deep Longing

The possibility of being liberated and transformed is what made our hearts beat a little faster as children when we read *Snow White*, played *Cinderella*, watched *Sleeping Beauty*, or sang along with *Little Mermaid*. Whether we costumed ourselves as brave heroes or as those rescued from a bind, we *identified* with these stories of redemption.

These classic fairy tale stories appeal to us because they touch a primal longing in our deep places by telling a story that is thoroughly true. Someone who's a lot like us is born into and enjoys royalty and/or privilege until a sudden tragedy jeopardizes his or her truest identity. This one, now cut off from loved ones, falls under the power of sin and death. Who will save him? Who will redeem her? The longing of the captive heart is that a saving face, with sufficient power to extricate us from our bind, will redeem and transform.

This is also the pattern that is deeply true of our lives.

Sprung free from the womb, our lives, for better or for worse, became a *function* of our parents or caregivers. But by virtue of the equation, we also appropriated their inherent sin and shame as our own. To live free, we must be liberated by one who is sinless and *[handwritten margin notes: "Accepts us as we are).", "Need to be someone we were not."]*

shameless. In Christ, our original negative condition—we strive futilely to live without sin and shame—is itself negated by the Prince of Peace. He takes on sin and shame and death to set us free.

In different words, this is the story the Church tells about what happens in our baptisms and at the Lord's Table. The protagonist—you or I—has been created to find identity and purpose in the context of a unique lineage. This person, though, falls from this intended condition into one of bondage where he or she is unable to extricate him- or herself from that which binds. The story climaxes as the protagonist is redeemed and reidentified—in baptism—by the gracious activity of a powerful mediator. This protagonist then experiences the ongoing process of receiving new life, through the continuing presence of the mediator—in the Eucharist—by which he or she is nourished and sustained in this new identity.

It's the story into which we're invited to live. In dying with Christ, our sin and death and shame are defeated. In this dramatic recentering of our being, we're regrounded and Christ lives in us. Christ acknowledges how our lives become a function of his life: "On that day you will realize that I am in my Father, and you are in me, and I am in you" (John 14:20 NIV).

[handwritten margin note: "Are we ?"]

In him we are received, fed, and sustained.

In him we experience the story that is deeply true.

The good news of the Christian gospel is that God's gracious face is turned toward ours in love. The chronic fear with which we live, that we will be found unacceptable by those we most need to receive us, has been defeated once and for all. In the life, death, and resurrection of Jesus—our heroic Prince of Peace—our lives have now become a function of the One whom the Father loves. Received by God through Christ, you and I—those who are undeniably beloved by the Father—simply *cannot* be abandoned or forsaken.

A Useless Cortex

Dr. Eben Alexander has experienced the kind of comprehensive liberation for which so many of us long. Caught in a bind from which he could not extricate himself, a deadly bacteria, he was set free by God to live a new life of radical freedom.

Though he would have called himself a Christian before his near-death experience, Alexander, a Harvard University neuro-surgeon, confesses that he was more so in name than by vir-tue of what he actually believed. He humbly shares, "I sympathized deeply with those who wanted to believe that there was a God somewhere out there who loved us unconditionally. In fact, I envied such people the security that those beliefs no doubt provided. But as a scientist, I simply knew better than to believe them myself."[1]

I've known people like this. Many of them are Christians. They long to see and hear and feel God's presence the way so many others claim to do, and they'd love to experience the fairy tale redemption, but they simply do not seem to have been *wired* to experience it. Though I don't know that being particularly intelligent *necessarily* clogs the spiritual circuits, there sometimes does appear to be some sort of loose correlation.

> The chronic fear with which we live, that we will be found unacceptable by those we most need to receive us, has been defeated once and for all.

When Alexander contracted a very rare bacterial meningitis, E. coli bacteria penetrated his cerebrospinal fluid and was, in his words, "eating" his brain. There was no scientific explanation, insists Alexander, for how—without brain function—he could experience a very vibrant type of consciousness as he journeyed to another world without the benefit of corporeal cooperation. And while most of the chief arguments *against* these types of near-death experiences depend on an assumption about a malfunction-ing cortex, Alexander's cortex wasn't malfunctioning. It was just —clinically speaking—*off*.

What Alexander reports experiencing when his cortex was not in operation was, in my opinion, a mixed bag. To my disappointment, his report included big, puffy, pink clouds and winged beings and glorious chanting. The reason I was disappointed in this part of the story is because I don't understand spiritual stuff like that when I read about it in the New Testament book of Revelation and I don't understand it when people like this guy bring reports back from the dead. I would have been much more comforted by a compelling description of a warm, sandy beach with an MP3 player and a full picnic basket—that I could have understood—but hey, it's his brain-death, not mine.

On his journey in this other world, Alexander had a guide. He describes the woman who traveled with him as a beautiful young woman in a simple peasant-style dress. (Note to self: fashion palette in the afterworld features powder blue, indigo, and pastel orange-peach. And though I have no basis for my keen intuition, this is not surprising me one bit.) What captured my imagination even more than the delicious palette, though, was Alexander's description of the way she *looked* at him.

"It was not a romantic look," he explains. "It was not a look of friendship. It was a look that was somehow beyond all these, beyond all the different compartments of love we have down here on earth."[2]

I thought he chose great words to describe something so entirely *other*.

In addition to "the look," there was a message.

Alexander reports that the message this attendant shared was spoken without words. He says the meaning sort of blew through him and convinced him of its veracity in its passing. Aware that this sounds unbelievably wispy, Alexander emphasizes the substantial and real nature of it. In a purposeful attempt to give words to the deep, compelling impression that was wordless, he translates the three parts of the message he received:

✓ "You are loved and cherished, dearly, forever."

✓ "You have nothing to fear."

? "There is nothing you can do wrong."[3]

164

If you're anything like me, upon reading those words you began frantically running each of these lines through your preexisting theology filter.

This is how they sounded as they ran through *my* filter: *I can live with "loved and cherished, dearly, forever." If this guy is one of God's elect—and it sure seems like he might be—then all of this is probably true.* I was reluctantly willing to believe that he, and we, are dearly loved.

I wonder if perhaps it means that there is nothing you can do to change the fact that you are, forever, dearly loved and cherished.

And if we believe, as we say we do, that all things are in God's hands, then—*technically*—there is probably nothing to fear. Probably.

But that last bit, that there's nothing he can do wrong, seems to fall out of bounds. Without batting an eye, I can think of a boatload of things he could do wrong. For starters, there are the Ten Commandments. He could do all those things wrong. And then there are all the other commandments. And I happen to know for a fact that there is a veritable plethora of things to do wrong today that hadn't even been invented yet when the Bible was written. So there are all those. Seriously, I could do this all day.

But since I'm giving this guy and his little journey the benefit of the doubt, I also feel compelled to open my mind to consider the *possibility* that the one he met, and the One I know, could really mean "There is nothing you can do wrong."

I won't lie: it's a little mind-bending. And though it feels far too liberal and loosey-goosey, it is also like coming up out of deep waters and gulping in gallons of fresh seaside air.

I wonder if perhaps it means that there is nothing you can do to change the fact that you are, forever, dearly loved and cherished. Or that anything you could possibly fear in this life or the next is over-whelmingly conquered by the reality of your eternal belovedness.

If it means those things, it means that God is more good than I can wrap my mind around.

Alexander encapsulates the message at the heart of his journey: "We are loved and accepted unconditionally by a God even more grand and unfathomably glorious than the one I'd learned of as a child in Sunday school."[4]

We are liberated, set free in so many ways, when we're accepted exactly as we are.

Alexander's experience raises again this beautiful and glorious question for each one of us: *Is it possible that God is more gracious than we've ever imagined?* Frankly, nothing about the doctor's encounter rules out the possibility that the One he encountered is of the same substance as Jesus and his dad. And isn't that just the most wonderful possibility?

- -

Do you long for the kind of comprehensive liberation that Dr. Alexander experienced? Or have you given up on the fairy tale possibility that God would set you free, in this lifetime, from the bind of both guilt and shame? Use your imagination to locate yourself in the story that is true: become a character in one of the stories recorded in the Gospels. Allow yourself to encounter Jesus, who so thoroughly liberated bodies, minds, and spirits. Where do you most need his touch today?

- -

15

Loved with the Same Stuff

My son Abhishek was three years old when he was baptized in a muddy pond in Hillsborough, North Carolina, during our church's annual fall picnic at Camp New Hope.

With our church family gathered on the shore as witnesses, Pastor Allan—with whom my husband Peter served in ministry—asked Peter and I if we trusted in Jesus Christ and if we'd raise Abhi to trust him too. After confirming our intention, Allan and Peter waded into the muddy waters, Peter holding small Abhi tightly in his arms.

Though we'd explained what would happen to three-year-old Abhi, we knew he didn't fully understand. As I stood on the shore, I felt sick. What kind of parents were we? Of course he'd be startled and scared. Was this abusive? It sure felt like it. Though everyone gathered ostensibly believed this baptism business was a good idea, I wondered which other witnesses were having the same concerns as I was. I knew that entire households were baptized in the first century, which certainly included three-year-olds, and with this I tried to soothe myself.

When he'd lumbered into water that was deep enough, Peter announced, "I baptize you in the name of the Father, the Son, and the Holy Spirit" and plunged under the water with Abhi.

They burst up together to the sounds of joyful clapping—Abhi predictably upset and Peter comforting him. Struggling against the muddy bottom, Peter brought him to the shore where I folded Abhi into my towel-ready arms. The anxiety that had welled up in my heart as I anticipated my child being plunged into fear, submerged under unfriendly waters, was the tiniest taste of reality. I had been asked to entrust my child to the care of the One who loved him more than Peter and I, believing that, in life and in death, Abhi was held in the loving arms of God.

> **Submitting to his father, Jesus demonstrated his confidence that, in life and in death, he was held in the loving arms of God.**

I'd put my faith in the hope that Abhi would be formed by the face—more reliable than the ones his father and I wore—of the Heavenly One who smiled upon him.

Baptism of Jesus

Over the years, as I've read about Jesus's baptism in the Jordan by his cousin John, I've felt confused and moved on quickly. What I knew of Christian baptism was that believers were washed clean of sin. What I knew of Jewish baptism, the kind John was performing, was that sinners could repent, turning from their sins. If Jesus was sinless, why did he get baptized?

The Gospel writer Matthew knew that his audience would be wondering what I wondered. I think this is why he portrays John as being just as befuddled by Jesus's request for baptism as I was.

"What? What?" John wondered. "That's whack! You should be baptizing me!"

Jesus reassured him, "Let it be so now; for it is proper for us in this way to fulfill all righteousness" (Matt. 3:15).

Matthew wanted us to know that, although it seemed nutty, Jesus's baptism was important.

So John consents, wades into the Jordan with Jesus, and does what so many boy-cousins playfully do to one another on hot summer days: he dunks him under the water.

What Happened?

Abhi had dipped below the waters dirty and, ostensibly—despite the gross pond scum—had come out spiritually cleaner.

If Jesus had gone in clean, though, then his baptism was about more than spiritual hygiene. It was about life and death. Under the waters he died. Up from the waters, he lived again. Submitting to his father, Jesus demonstrated his confidence that, in life and in death, he was held in the loving arms of God.

The image of clean Jesus being dunked clean sort of begs the question of who the primary "audience" was for Jesus's baptism. If Jesus wasn't being made clean for God, was the ritual for our benefit? Was it for *us*? As a parent, I don't make my kids take a bath if they're already squeaky clean. I might, however, drag a comb through their hair before I drop them off to go to the symphony with their grandparents. That is not for my benefit, nor my children's. It is for their *grandparents'* benefit. They're the audience for the big comb show. Similarly, I'm more likely to believe that the party needing to recognize Jesus's acceptability and chosenness was a human audience and not a divine one. I'm prone to believe that, in an act fueled by God's great love, we became privileged to divine mystery at Jesus's baptism. For the crowd gathered on the shore of the Jordan, and those of us across the centuries who continue to bear witness to the life of Jesus, the baptism of Jesus was a *meaning-making* event. In it, Jesus stood in solidarity with those of us who go in dirty and come out clean. It prefigured his death and resurrection, as well as ours.

But the event also *identified* Jesus to us in a very particular way. For starters, he was identified as *Messiah*.

The One Who Was Fully Received

For centuries, the Jews had waited for the Messiah. They longed and hoped for the one to come, the one Isaiah had identified as God's servant. And, over that time, any number of likely candidates had seemed as though they might fit the bill as the one who would redeem Israel. But this guy, claimed the Gospel writers, was the real deal. Jesus's baptism was the inaugural event announcing, "This is the one!"

Most of us today don't hear it, at first blush, in the text. "Just as he came up from the water," Matthew explains, "suddenly the heavens were opened to him and he saw the Spirit of God descending like a dove and alighting on him. And a voice from heaven said, 'This is my Son, the Beloved, with whom I am well pleased'" (Matt. 3:16–17).

For the first-century Jewish audience, the words wafting from the heavens, "This is my Son," would have echoed with the words God had spoken over the anointed King of Israel, David. Naming Jesus as *beloved*—reminiscent of endearments used for Solomon and Benjamin—identified him as God's chosen. Identifying Jesus as the one "with whom I am well pleased" evoked Isaiah's prophecy of God's chosen one who was to come.

In every way, the Gospel writers were referencing the Jews' shared historical memory, identifying Jesus as the one chosen by God to redeem the world God loved. They tagged him so that anyone searching the Scriptures for #Messiah would be pointed to Jesus. And their telling of Jesus's baptism—the upside-down equivalent of a king's anointing, turning power upside down and foreshadowing the defeat of death—was intended to do just that.

This Other Thing

Yes, Jesus's baptism was a meaning-making event identifying him as the Messiah. It is how the story is meant to function in the canon of Scripture.

170

But there's this other thing. It begins quietly at Jesus's baptism, gathers momentum throughout his ministry, and climaxes when Jesus shares with his disciples at the end of his life. This other thing is the Father's *love* for Jesus. Yes, he's chosen. Yes, he's sent. Yes, he's used to redeem. But he's also *loved*. Though it's certainly all tangled up with his Messiah-ness, the Father's love for Jesus is this other beautiful theme throughout the Gospels.

In that holy moment, those who were gathered on the muddy shore of the Jordan were given a glimpse into the relationship between Father and Son. With their eyes, they saw the heavens open. They saw something that looked like a dove, recognizable as God's Spirit, descending and landing on Jesus. With their ears, they heard a heavenly voice announce, "This is my Son, the Beloved, with whom I am well pleased."

With their eyes they could see that God was *with* Jesus. With their ears they could hear that God was *for* Jesus.

In that moment, Jesus was *received* the way we all long to be received.

Jesus is marked, in a very singular way, as the one God loves. He's named as the one in whom God delights. In increasing measure, Jesus is identified as belonging to God, being loved by God, and even being the object of God's delight.

> Yes, he's chosen. Yes, he's sent. Yes, he's used to redeem. But he's also *loved.*

This anointing of God's servant isn't simply a functional transaction, the hire and commission of a guy who could get the job done. That would sound more like, "This is my agent, the capable one, who can get a job done." I'm not knocking that possibility, either. If I had that reference, I'd be thrilled to put it on my own résumé. But at his baptism, Jesus is identified, in a very particular way, as one who is *loved*.

Eugene Peterson paraphrases Matthew 3:17 as, "This is my Son, chosen and marked by my love, delight of my life" (Message).

The Father *delighted* in the Son.

My Jesus Musings

I'm of the mind that, by the time of his baptism, Jesus already *knew* himself to be fully received by the Father. He wasn't wondering about it. It wasn't a question for him, the way it can be for us. Though he would have seen the same kinds of faces you and I did as a child—a mother who was exhausted, a dad who was worried about his business, subsequent siblings who would despise his firstborn status—Jesus had also been uniquely formed by the face of his heavenly Father.

Though Jesus's first thirty years are woefully sparse in historical detail, we get a wonderful peek at this very thing in twelve-year-old Jesus at the temple. His whole family and community had made their annual road trip to Jerusalem for the Festival of the Passover. The way a few families traveling together today—to the beach or fourth of July fireworks or a campground—might gather up all of their things and head back to the car in one big mob, so too Jesus's family was traveling home in a big pack of folks. Assuming Jesus was running around with his friends and cousins, Mary and Joseph eventually discovered he was gone. Rushing back to Jerusalem, it took them three days to find him! When they did, he was in the temple, engaged with the teachers there. Everyone who heard him was floored by his understanding.

> The descending dove and the heavenly voice were for *us*. They are what *we needed* to understand the love Jesus's Father had for him.

As a parent of three children about Jesus's age—now eleven, twelve, and thirteen—it's hard for me to get past the part about thinking it's okay to "check out" for three days. When I do, though, I'm left looking at a boy who was *grounded* in a very particular way. He amazed the teachers in the temple with his understanding. The implication was that Jesus had impressed the teachers with the maturity of his wisdom. His questions and his answers revealed a depth of knowing that amazed those who had gathered to hear him.

Remarkably, Jesus doesn't appear to grasp why his folks would be so panicked. "Why were you searching for me? Did you not know that I must be in my Father's house?" (Luke 2:49). As a parent, a response like this from an ordinary child would likely result in some sort of disciplinary action. Yet Joseph and Mary, despite their confusion, do not institute a punishment. Rather, the writer Luke quickly notes that Jesus dutifully joined them for the return to Nazareth and was obedient to them.

Any way you slice it, this is such a weird moment, right?

When I strip it of all the weird parental anxieties and fury that I bring to it, I see a kid who seems to genuinely understand himself as one who is identified by someone he knows as Father. Yes, I assume Jesus has been shaped, in some degree, by the parents God chose for him, but he really understands himself as *belonging*, in a very formative way, to the Father he's encountered at the temple.

A Holy Announcement

Now, fast-forward eighteen years to Jesus's baptism, when a voice trumpets from heaven, "This is my Son, the Beloved, with whom I am well pleased" (Matt. 3:17).

This announcement of belovedness *could* have been received by Jesus as a quiet impression he could have simply experienced in the quiet of his heart during his baptism. That he knew himself to be the son of a heavenly Father, whom he knew intimately and was also known by, was so evident, even during his childhood, that it's safe to believe he already knew himself to be God's beloved.

The descending dove and the heavenly voice were for *us*. They are what *we needed* to understand the love Jesus's Father had for him.

Throughout the Gospels—in the family temple debacle, as Jesus steals off privately to pray, when he teaches his friends to pray, when he monologues at the end of his life about how much his Father loves him—we are allowed to peek at the kind of relationship with a heavenly Father for which *we* were made. All of that could have, and no doubt did, happen internally, within Jesus. But the one who came to show us the way to the Father and to *be* the way to the Father wants us to see and hear and know that this is all for us. The dove and the voice at Jesus's baptism, designed to be perceived by human eyes and human ears, were for *our* benefit. They identified Jesus to us because Jesus already knew himself to be God's beloved. Jesus shows us what it is to live as one who is *entirely* received by the Father.

With these eyes that search for authentic affection, I survey the Gospels to discover what God's relationship to Jesus was like. Specifically, I'm curious to know if there was genuine *affection* between them. And I *do* hear echoes of it in the text.

I recognize twelve-year-old Jesus's absurdly intimate identification with one he knows as Father.

I hear the words spoken at Jesus's baptism, "This is my Son, the Beloved, with whom I am well pleased."

I notice Jesus sneaking away from his friends to share time with the Father.

I hear Jesus's insistence to doubters that his Father is with him and for him.

I can't help but observe that Jesus knows himself to be *loved* by the Father.

From these clues I've gathered, it seems as though Jesus experiences the posture of God toward him to be one of intimacy, affection, delight, sharing, security, concern, and care. And that posture was crystallized, and most clearly articulated, in the words spoken at Jesus's baptism.

The Same Stuff

God's gracious posture toward Jesus begs the question of God's posture toward you and me. Is it, as early church father Origen theorized, that of a helpless God unable to defeat Satan without trickery? Is it, as Anselm suggested in the eleventh century, an angry

God demanding his due? Or could it be, per thirteenth-century Aquinas and sixteenth-century Calvin, that God's justice demands that someone be punished?

As Jesus gives his friends a final round of admonition and instruction before his crucifixion, he posits something that's a little outrageous: "As the Father has loved me," he insists, "so I have loved you; abide in my love" (John 15:9).

Jesus is saying that the love his Father has for him is the love Jesus has for his followers. It's the *same stuff*. Specifically, the love that the Father had for Jesus at his baptism is the *same* love with which Christ loves us.

A voice in me protests, *Wait, wait, it can't be. Those nice baptism words were spoken over the* Messiah, *God's holy chosen one, and I'm just . . . me. Let's not confuse the Savior with the saved!*

But it's the same stuff.

Jesus wanted his disciples to know that God's gracious loving posture toward him at his baptism is God's posture toward us.

Try these words on for size: "This is my child, the beloved, with whom I am well pleased." Do they fit you?

The face tipped toward Jesus at his baptism is a face that is entirely gracious.

It is the face that is tipped toward you today.

· ·

The love the Father has for the Son is the same stuff with which God loves you. Pretty amazing, huh? Take some time to meditate on the Father's words in Matthew 3:17, "This is my Son, the Beloved, with whom I am well pleased." While you are admittedly not the Messiah, can you hear and receive echoes of God's love that is **for** you?

· ·

16

Jennifer, Boy, Boy, and Boy

hat's like watching a newspaper."

"The worst thing is reading the Bible book."

"It's wet!"

Without context, words strung together can mean very little.

Tiny Wordbearers

When my first child started babbling, I used a little notebook to write down things she said. I'd listen in, via wireless monitor, to her early morning conversations with the stuffed animals in her crib as she'd boss them around like she was herding them into her vehicle, telling them to put on their seatbelts.

As she grew, and was joined by two brothers, I continued to write down the funny things they said. In fact, for a number of years I'd publish annual updates for the grandparents. I have no idea if these witticisms are as funny to others as they are to me, having been there, but they really make me so happy.

For instance, when she was six, Zoe asked me about the first movie ever. I explained to her about silent moving pictures, explaining, "The first movies didn't even have sound."

She queried, "Were they black and gray?"

"Yes! They were!" I applauded.

Turning to her little brother, earnest Zoe, the consummate instructor, explained to him, "Rollie, that's like watching a newspaper."

That's funny.

About the same time, when Rollie was four, I asked him to dictate a note for me to include in my thanks to his Sunday school teacher.

Rollie started strong with, "The worst thing is reading the Bible book, just sitting around."

Thankfully, it got better after that.

During the dicey toilet-training season, my youngest would usually wake up with wet pajama bottoms. And tops. And sheets. And blankets. And toys. Sometimes carpet. One morning, with more pride than was merited, Abhi peeled off his wet Buzz Lightyear pajama bottoms and proudly announced, "It's wet! But only on da inside and da outside!"

Fabulous, right?

With the context and my adoring commentary, you know a little bit more about what the words meant and who spoke them.

You can know that Zoe, at age six, is already a teacher.

You can know that Rollie isn't trying to impress anyone with an eloquent note.

You can know that Abhi is sweet and earnest.

Without ever meeting my kiddos, you can learn something about them from the words they speak and the context in which they're spoken.

Some Things You Can't Know

If you don't know the context, it's hard to pick up the meaning.

For instance, if you thought Zoe was a disgruntled teenager, you might have thought that describing a movie as being like watching a newspaper might have been some sour jab about how bad the movie was.

If you thought Rollie was twenty-three, him saying something like "Bible book" might have led you to believe that English wasn't his first language.

If you thought Abhi might be a sneaky fibber, then his hedging about how wet his pants actually were would sound more cunning than the earnest and innocent intentions with which he spoke.

From the words spoken, you can know a *little* something about the speaker, but—from just the words—you could also be way off the mark.

Sadly, this happens too often in church. While God's written Word is a true gift to the church, its delivery may or may not be.

If every Sunday morning we heard the words of Scripture delivered by an angry old elder, then Jesus's voice through the pages of the Gospels, as heard in our ears and hearts, might sound kind of angry.

If we had a religious grandmother who shamed us, insisting that God was keeping close track of our sins, then we may have heard the most benign words of Jesus as shaming ones.

But if we were irreligious until we hit rock bottom and ended up encountering God in the faces and voices of friends in Alcoholics Anonymous, Jesus might have a very understanding face and forgiving tone.

Or if we were raised in a church with a pastor who knew her- or himself to be a sinner, and knew Jesus to be full of grace and mercy, the voice of Jesus in our ears and in our hearts might be one that is deliciously kind.

The ways in which the words of Jesus are given life in our ears and heads and hearts—whether they ring with compassion or judgment or anger or hope—are what endow them with meaning.

Holy Macaroni

A number of years ago, when I worshiped at a church in an impoverished village in Ensenada, Mexico, I'd not yet taken any lessons or classes to learn Spanish. Sitting in the congregation, however, taking in the preacher's message, I could tell without a shadow of a doubt that what he was saying was *good* news. The message itself was communicated in his delivery: his joy-filled eyes and his hope-filled expression. From the person, from the delivery, I intuited: good news.

The fact is, he could have been saying "Jesus is a piece of macaroni," and had he paused for the congregation to respond I would have shouted "Amen, *hermano*!" The message itself, the good news, was borne by him in such a way that it was received as true and efficacious.

In case it's not clear, this delivery thing is very important to me. The tone, volume, and inflection we give to language *communicates* its meaning.

Sadly, this happens too often in church. While God's written Word is a true gift to the church, its delivery may or may not be.

Though I wish I could give some noble reason, it may just be that I come from a Vaudeville people. I do, by blood, through the line of my paternal grandmother. We're performers. I don't mean performers in the inauthentic "posing" way, but performers in the most authentic way, delivering a message with integrity by giving face and voice that vivify it. Perhaps I think too highly of myself and my performing ancestors. I'm convinced, however, that the way in which the message is delivered matters deeply. In fact, I'm convinced that the delivery actually *becomes* the message itself.

Jennifer, Boy, Boy, and Boy

My cousin's name is Jennifer. If she pops into her mom's house unannounced, my Aunt Susan might shout, "Jennifer!" with as much enthusiasm as if Jennifer were the Queen of England. The way she welcomes her, you simply can't stand by watching and not want to *be* Jennifer.

I've also got a friend named Jennifer. When she would get in trouble as a child, if she worked a little mischief, her mother would speak her name, dripping with venom, as if it were shameful. Jennifer reports, "The way she said *Jennifer* was as if I, myself, was a scandal."

Delivery matters.

To grasp the meaning and nature and tone of Jesus's words for us, we need to listen for the voice that is authentic to him.

You may not know a Jennifer, but I am certain you know a boy. *Boy* is a great word in which to listen for the different tones various speakers bring to a word.

Andrew P. Morrison had an aunt who never called him by his name. When she'd inquire about him with his parents, she'd always call him "the boy." For Morrison, who felt deeply loved and cherished by his aunt, the word *boy* dripped with affection.

When young men join the gang life, they may refer to their associates in this new type of family as their "boys." To identify someone on the street as "my boy" is to say that they *belong* to one another.

In the southern United States, slave owners used the word *boy* to describe grown men whom they considered to be their property. Diminutive, devaluing, this same word stripped men of human dignity.

Secret Service agent Jerry Parr describes the way in which the wife of Vice President Spiro Agnew recognized the humanity of the silent, serious, homogenous, dark-suited agents who protected her family. She would offer one a sandwich or visit with their wives or persuade their boss to let them come in from the rain. Parr reports, "She called the agents 'my boys' and none of us seemed to mind."[1]

As men gather weapons and supplies in preparation for war, a twelve-year-old begs his father to take him along. With respect and compassion, the father denies him, saying, "You're just a boy."

After trying for years to conceive, a husband stands by his wife's side as she labors to bring forth their first child. Early ultrasounds indicated they'd be bringing home a girl. As the newborn nurses at his mother's breast, the father steals into the hospital waiting room, where grandparents, aunts, uncles, and cousins have gathered, and bursts out, "It's a boy!"

One word, riddled with different meanings. In each, it is the speaker that gives particular meaning to the same word.

Different Tones for Different Folks

Most of us have heard the words of Jesus delivered by others in all manner of different voices: warm and cool, forgiving and condemning, passionate and disinterested. To grasp the meaning and nature and tone of Jesus's words for us, we need to listen for the voice that is *authentic to him.*

Some of us, who suspect that Jesus was a pretty serious fellow, might be dying to hear an affectionately warm tone from his lips. We long to hear kindness in the words he speaks to prostitutes and tax collectors and fishermen and to us.

Some of us, though, *won't* want to hear a warm affectionate Mrs. Agnew–tone echoing in the voice of Jesus. We are dead certain that Jesus was—at least in part—angry and condemning. Which is not entirely wrong. The Gospels bear witness to moments when Jesus's countenance and voice were full of fire and fury. But if Jesus's "angry voice" is to have any real meaning, it's imperative that we pay attention to who was on the receiving end of it.

Those who were on the receiving end of Jesus's angry voice were the ones who insisted on their own rightness, perseverating on pointing out the guilt and brokenness and shamefulness of others. Among these, Jesus's language and tone clearly communicated his intolerance for injustice.

Jesus was furious about the ways the behavior of the Pharisees and teachers of the law had shut the door to God in the faces of others. He's angry that their ruse of religious rightness, offering just the right gifts at the temple, had blinded them to the more important matters of justice, mercy, and faithfulness. He hated that they looked righteous on the outside but were full of greed, self-indulgence, hypocrisy, and wickedness. He's brokenhearted that rather than welcoming God's prophets, the Religious had, instead, killed them.

Remember the various "types" of God-faces revealed by the Baylor University study? The Pharisees experienced a face in Jesus that was *near*—right up in their grills, most likely—and was also *angry*. The question raised in my mind is whether or not Jesus was *for* them in those angry moments. Some would see it differently than I do, but I'm of the mind that he was so very passionately *for* them that he wanted them to wake up and live into the reality of who God was, who they were, and who others were.

There's no question, however, that when the self-righteous Religious were addressed by Jesus, they heard a tone that expressed God's holy anger.

The *unrighteous*, though, heard a very different tone in Jesus's voice. The tone he used with social outcasts, those who knew themselves to be guilty and broken and shameful, was, more often than not, full of grace. His compassionate voice surprised—and even offended!—those who heard it.

Jesus did not mark others as "in" or "out" of the club based on whatever religious affiliation cards they carried in their pockets. Rather, Jesus revealed the *measure* God uses in the story he told about two guys who went to pray. You're "in," said Jesus, if you recognize your sin and brokenness. I'd paraphrase to say that you're "in" when you're in touch with what's real. You're "out," said Jesus, if you deny your sin and brokenness. You're "out" when, out of touch with *what is*, you mask up.

The Voice That Is True

One way to reach back through the centuries, to really listen for the authentic sound and tone and kindness of Jesus's voice, is to notice the *responses* of those who heard it. From our own experiences we know that a voice of judgment and condemnation shuts people down—or ignites their anger—and a voice filled with grace and welcome opens people up.

To a sinful woman standing beside a well, Jesus's compassionate voice not only opened her heart to truth and grace, it compelled her to tell all her friends about him.

Zacchaeus, a dirty, no-good tax collector, heard a voice of invitation that was filled with graciousness. What Zacchaeus heard in that voice, and saw on Jesus's face, moved him and transformed him.

The voice heard by Levi, another tax collector, wasn't one that wedged him further into hardened vice. Rather, Jesus's invitation was filled with such gracious welcome that it released Levi from his lucrative, exploitive ways.

Jesus does not wear a false, cheery, anything-goes mask, with voice to match, nor does he wear the shaming mask we've sometimes given him. Rather, he is abundantly gracious to those who recognize their need for grace, and decidedly firm with those who exploit the vulnerable.

In Jesus's day, what had been communicated to the weak and brokenhearted by the Religious was *shame*. The collective voice of the Religious had insisted that the sinful were not good enough to be received by God. Whether by virtue of disability or shameful profession or religion or race or specific sin, the self-righteous Religious had, with an ugly tone, rejected the unrighteous.

Jesus's gracious tone, in the ears of the rejected, was like healing balm. Without a hint of shame—you're not good enough, you're not welcome, you're not received, you don't belong—the tone of Jesus's voice expressed just the opposite. Those who were *unacceptable* were accepted by Jesus.

Some of the dissonance we can find in the text, as modern readers, may give us clues about the chilly or hard tone we've unintentionally assigned to Jesus. For example, some of the points at which we say, "What on earth just happened, and why?" become more comprehensible when we mute the harsh religious voice we've given to Jesus and allow him, instead, to speak with gracious compassion. When we do, the fact that Levi jumps up and follows Jesus no longer feels impulsive and sudden and confusing. That a disreputable tax collector would scramble out of a tree at the sound of Jesus's voice makes *more* sense. That a woman whose sins have been detailed runs to tell her town about Jesus seems less absurd.

Try this approach at home! Notice the difference in another person when you use a bitter, judging tone and when you use a generous, gracious one. When we begin to hear the tone of Jesus's voice among sinners and to see the expression on his face as full of God's steadfast love and compassion, the text itself makes more sense.

> **When we begin to hear the tone of Jesus's voice among sinners and to see the expression on his face as full of God's steadfast love and compassion, the text itself makes more sense.**

As you tip your ears toward the One who is gracious, listen for the fullness of who God is to echo throughout his grace-filled words to you.

When you listen for God's voice, speaking to you through Scripture or in prayer, how does it sound? Do you hear judgment, disappointment, or condemnation? (Note: in some moments, these might be appropriate to hear!) More often, however, are you able to hear gracious, unconditional love and acceptance for you exactly as you are? Listen, now, for the voice that is gracious.

17

The Face of
Infinite Compassion

Dr. Mary Neal, former director of spine surgery at the University of Southern California, was too busy for God. Though she believed in God, the life she shared with her husband and four children was too full to make spirituality a priority.

In 1999, Dr. Neal was kayaking in southern Chile. After cascading down a waterfall, her kayak became submerged underwater. The force of the rushing water was so great her body was flattened to the front deck of the boat. Unable to extricate herself, Dr. Neal—who *was* willing to pray for help when the chips were down—asked for God's will to be done.

With some of the group above the falls and some having passed over it, no one knows exactly how long Dr. Neal had been submerged when the leader of the group confirmed her absence. When rescuers began to hunt for her, however, one started a timer on his watch. Fifteen minutes later, they found Mary's body.

They found her *dead*.

Yes, yes, another story like this. Spoiler alert: she's dead and she's going to be brought back to life. Guilty. I'm a sucker for these stories because so often they offer a glimpse of the voice and face and presence of the One for whom we long. So, enjoy.

Mary herself describes what she experienced before she was found. When her body had stopped functioning, Mary says that she was greeted by a group of spirits who "looked like compassion, even though that's not an adjective."[1]

Dr. Neal felt as though she were going home.

When they extracted her from the river, however, her rescuers had other plans.

One kept calling to Dr. Neal to come back and take a breath. She admits that she was pretty irritated with him, because she was in a *good place*. She had left, she was home, and—despite his insistence—she had no plans to come back.

On the *Today Show*, when Matt Lauer asked *why*, Dr. Neal explained, "Because I felt absolutely like I was home . . . it was my absolute true home." She continued, "I was absolutely overwhelmed with this physical sensation of being held, and comforted and reassured." And of the spirits who served as her guides, she explained, "Not only did these beings explode with this incredible love, but they took me down this exceptionally beautiful path toward this sort of great dome structure of sorts."

Knowing how these life-after-death stories go, Matt ventured, "You met Jesus?"

Humbly, Mary admitted, "I feel very presumptuous saying that, but I believe that Jesus was holding me when I was still in my boat and reassuring me and comforting me."

I was grateful when Matt asked exactly the question I was itchy to ask her: "Did Jesus look like the image of Jesus we have all come to know?"

"He didn't look like the image in my Sunday school books, no," she revealed. "But again, I would say that I didn't look at him critically, in terms of saying what color was the hair. I looked at him and what I saw was infinite kindness and compassion."[2]

That infinite kindness and compassion is the *face* of Jesus.

The Face of Jesus

The conversation reminded me of the various renderings of Jesus I've seen in museums and magazines and textbooks. In fact, a few months ago I was pawing through magazines at the local reuse warehouse when I came across the December 1994 *Life* magazine featuring Jesus on the cover. Though the article itself, a collection of thoughts from scholars and respected religious personalities, was sort of stale, the *images* that *Life* featured were fantastic—portraits of Jesus from artists around the globe, each featuring Jesus in the skin of various people groups. So, in addition to blue-eyed European American Jesus, there was also Chinese Jesus, Haitian Jesus, Russian Jesus, and more!

Mary Neal did not register Jesus's particular features in her encounter because that is not what mattered most—just as what matters most about these works, in my opinion, is what is communicated by the particular face an artist has portrayed. From my slim survey of artistically rendered Jesuses, what I've seen most often communicated is *serene disinterest*. In far too many statues, paintings, and sketches, there is no indication that there is any *life* inside Jesus. He's not glad or sad or mad or afraid. He's neither hot nor icy. He's tepidly cool . . . lukewarm. The void of affect, perhaps a creative attempt to portray him as more than human, ultimately portrays him as *less* than human. The stoic, serene detachment simply does not match the person described in the Gospel accounts.

Specifically, of the sixteen popular Jesuses from around the world portrayed in *Life*, not one was someone I'd want to chat with on the sidelines of a soccer game. While not all of them had that half-dead, constipated expression, none of them depicted a person who drew people to himself. Honestly, if I saw any of these guys sitting in the bleachers at my kid's American *futbol* game on Saturday morning, I'd want to climb a few rows higher to keep a safe distance.

The rendering that looked the most familiar to me was the dead serious, oil-painted European American Jesus. This guy, whom I've seen framed in countless church hallways, has brown, shoulder-length hair and a matching beard. He has flawless skin, which I envy. A halo of light is behind his head. His serene eyes, staring into the distance, are tilted upward.

Painted Haitian Jesus looked both confused and a bit desperate, as if he'd been caught in a crack house and was searching for an exit.

Baby Korean Jesus and adult Chinese Jesus both had their heads tipped, humbly, downward toward the ground.

The way in which Jesus is given a face in our hearts and minds communicates the way we understand who he is in relation to others and in relation to us.

Painted Russian icon Jesus looked like he'd been crying. For the last twenty-one centuries.

Carved West African Jesus appeared as though he might be suffering from clinical depression and in need of both therapy *and* a good antidepressant. Inked Mexican Indian Jesus too.

Oil-painted African American Jesus appeared concerned about the needs of a hurting world, and he also looked like he might be a tad bit ticked off.

Not so for grey, stone Swedish Jesus. His wide-eyed, vacant stare and ever-so-slightly upturned lips suggested he'd bottled up any negative feelings he might have buried in his stone heart.

Carved, wooden Filipino Jesus and painted Mexican Jesus both had their eyes closed. Iron-cast, bare-breasted female Jesus did too.

Now, I realize that, by virtue of their necessary limitations, no image can tell the *whole* story of a person.

And yet, in the necessary act of giving a human face to a man we've never seen, locating a visual representation of him in our hearts and minds, we pin *one* of these inadequate masks to the God-man. The way in which Jesus is given a face in our hearts and minds communicates the way we understand who he is in relation to others and in relation to us.

Not a Shopkeeper Who's Just Been Burglarized

For whatever personal or religious reasons, too often we've given Jesus the face of a sourpuss. Whether we're reading the text aloud in worship, or giving Jesus a voice inside our heads, there's no indication—in his face or voice or person—that this man is *for* us.

The story of Jesus being smashed about by an unwieldy crowd, where a bleeding woman touches the hem of his garment and is healed, has always, in my memory, had Jesus seeming a little *angry*. Whoever read the story, in my hearing or in my head, had conveyed Jesus as stern, mad that someone sneak-touched his clothes and sucked power out of him on the down low. He looked and sounded the way I sound when one of my kids has been riffling through my closet and garments that used to be on hangers are left in a crumpled heap on the floor.

"Hey! Who touched my clothes?" (see Mark 5:30).

Jesus and I are both put out that someone had the nerve to touch our garments without our permission.

Just once I'd love to hear someone in church read it, and tell it *with their face*, as if this touch-healing was a science experiment Jesus had been trying to perfect for a while and it *finally* worked! When he felt the power leave him, Jesus just knew someone had been healed and he wanted to confirm it.

With a big grin he'd ask, loud enough for everyone around to hear, "Hey, guys! Who touched my clothes? Which one of you is it, because I want to make sure you're *completely* well! Isn't this fantastic?"

Truth is, it probably did *not* happen like that. I suspect this because Mark reports that the healed woman was terrified as she confessed that she'd been the one. Whether she was scared of the real Jesus or of a powerful healer whom she'd just robbed isn't clear.

So let's say Jesus wasn't the happy mad scientist, but was just taken off-guard by the exchange, and he *doesn't* respond with a joyful, happy face.

When the woman, trembling, falls down before him, he doesn't reprimand her. He doesn't ask for the power back. He doesn't treat her like a thief. He blesses her!

The affectionate term *daughter* points to tenderness. It hardly seems possible to maintain a stern face while saying, "Daughter, your faith has made you well; go in peace, and be healed of your disease" (Mark 5:34). Somehow, though, standing behind a pulpit and reading Scripture *very seriously* seems to draw stern-voice out of many of us.

With the eyes of my heart, though, I see Jesus's face dripping with tender affection for a sufferer who has been set free. In fact, it *delights* him.

That, right there, is the face of God.

Not Treating His Friend Like a Numbskull

In the same way Jesus is too often voiced by readers as being irritated that he got power-sucked, I've heard "Jesus" use this same irritated tone with Mary Magdalene after his resurrection.

In John's telling of resurrection morning, Mary is ready to prepare the body for burial and is weeping outside the tomb. When she looks inside, she sees two angels who scold her for weeping. When she tells these angels that someone has taken Jesus's body and she can't find him, she turns around to see Jesus standing there. But—whether in shock or simply because of shadows—she doesn't recognize him. In fact, she thinks he's the *gardener*. Which, to her credit I think, makes way more earthly sense than "risen Savior" would. I think we can cut her some slack on that one.

So many readers I've heard reading Jesus's words here give him a tone that sounds a little disappointed—with a teeny dash of disgust. The voice they give to Jesus makes it sound as though Mary really should have recognized him. The readers' faces, of course, match their tone.

"Woman," too many half-accuse, "why are you weeping? Whom are you looking for?"

Like she did with the angels, Mary tells Jesus that she's looking for *Jesus*.

In reply, he says just one word.

He says, "*Mary.*"

For years I'd always heard it—from the voices of others as well as myself—as if it meant "silly girl." And what's communicated in this type of reading is, "Mary, come on! I can't believe you didn't know it was me."

And while it certainly sounds very much like the way I'd speak to my cousin if she were swimming in the ocean without her glasses and didn't recognize me at first, it doesn't sound anything like the man who really *loves* his disciples and knows that Mary and the gang are about to get the most awesome surprise of their lives.

I'm of the mind that it happened more as if Mary had glanced at the caller ID on her ringing cell, thought it was a telemarketer, and, distracted, answered it anyway. She thinks she's talking to a faceless worker she doesn't know—but the voice on the other end is her brother, who was just unexpectedly released from death row! Mary didn't think she'd ever see him again! The familiar voice—obviously emitting from a face that is beaming—says, "Mary! It's me! You know me, girl. It's your brother!"

The face of God isn't shaming us for being . . . human. Instead, it lights up, eliciting our gaze and affection, as one who already knows us and loves us.

That, right there, is the face of God.

Clearing Up a Mysterious Misunderstanding

In the period preceding his crucifixion, when Jesus knows his time is growing short, he rounds up the disciples and hunkers down with them for final instructions. Much of it appears to go right over the disciples' heads. And to be fair to them, it did sound a little bit like crazy talk.

Philip has been tracking along as Jesus has been promising to prepare a place for them at his Father's house. Making what, in my opinion, is a very reasonable request, Philip says, "Lord, show us the Father, and we will be satisfied" (John 14:8).

With the hindsight of centuries of theology, the Religious among us smugly know that Jesus is preparing for his friends a heavenly home, and that his dad is of an order they don't quite fathom. These folks act as if it's actually *quite* fathomable, and I've most often heard this passage read as if Philip, like the bleeding woman and like Mary, is getting a good scolding when Jesus replies, "Have I been with you all this time, Philip, and you still do not know me?" (v. 9). If you listen closely you can almost hear the other eleven breathe a deep sigh of relief that they weren't boneheaded enough to have asked the question they were *all* thinking.

Too often, the modern reader says it the same way I reiterate my children's chores each evening, the same ones they've been doing for years, when they pretend like they have no idea that dishes get rinsed, floors get swept, and cat poop gets scooped. The Jesus-voice I most often hear in worship gatherings today is one that shames Philip for asking a question to which he really should have known the answer, had he been paying attention.

This scolding voice nags, "Have I been with you all this time, Philip, and you still do not know me? DUH!" The berating continues as Jesus states the *obvious*, "Whoever has seen me has seen the Father" (v. 9). The bit goes on further, in John's telling, usually with more shaming from a Religious reader: "How can you say, 'Show us the Father'? Do you not believe . . ." (vv. 9–10).

And yet could it not be that, as in the garden with Mary, Jesus was glad for the opportunity to reveal himself and might have had a little smile on his face because he had this terrific opportunity to reveal himself—reveal his Father—to his friends?

"It's me! It's me!"

My Own Complicity

I know I talk about these churchy Scripture-readers as if *they're* the numbskulls for voicing Jesus as if he thinks everyone *else* is a numbskull. Please, please know that I count myself in these ranks. Too often, this is exactly how Jesus's voice sounds in my own head:

put out that he has to explain all this stuff that is so . . . plain. I think readers like me are communicating Jesus the way we've heard him communicated to us.

When I purpose to entertain another possibility, though, I imagine that Jesus is the kind of math tutor who really loves math and really loves people who don't get math. I've seen this delighted expression on the face of my genius daughter when she gets to help someone else with math. It's really clear, from her face and her voice, that she gets a lot of pleasure from helping people with math. That the other student might begin the tutoring session by not understanding a concept does not ruffle Zoe's proverbial feathers one bit. Fired up, passionate, she just uses more words, different words, to help engage them with the delightful *wonder* of awesome math.

I think that's the kind of teacher Jesus is.

So when the bleeding woman or Mary or Philip clearly are not understanding the equation, Jesus—sort of excited, like my Zoe—simply explains further, because he really *wants* each one to get it. Because he loves math. And he loves these precious ones. And he knows how much getting the math is going to help them.

In Philip's case, the face that loves him and loves math inches his understanding along, beaming, "This is not an easy one, but we've been working toward it for a while, bro. It's the transitive property, remember? You've got this one, Phil. You already know that I'm the One who's been sent, and if you remember that the One who's been sent is the same stuff as the Sender, then you know that I'm the spitting image of my dad. Awesome, right?"

> **I think readers like me are communicating Jesus the way we've heard him communicated to us.**

That is a much different voice from the Phil-you're-an-imbecile voice, isn't it?

That, right there, is the face of God.

I could do this *all day long*. The face of God that is tipped toward the diseased and confused and scared and confounded and sinful is simply not a mirror of the ones we're used to seeing. Choose any Gospel story in the Bible, stand in front of a mirror, and read it with the shaming voice. Make your fake shame-Jesus sound as bad and condescending and belittling and judgmental as you want. Whoever is listening in on your weird exercise from the hallway should feel like a worthless piece of dirt when you're done.

Hopefully, that eavesdropper will stick around for round two. Repeat the exact same words with the most kind and gracious voice you can muster. Channel whoever you have to—your sweet grandmother or your kindergarten teacher or Glinda the Good Witch—and allow Jesus's voice to ring with compassion and kindness.

And if you are hungry to be received by a face that accepts you exactly as you are, allow the face of Jesus—the true face, not the one we've given him—to glow with holy compassion for you.

Skim through the Gospels and look for the words of Jesus. Use your imagination to see Jesus's face and hear Jesus's voice speaking the printed words. First, imagine the words spoken with ugly, condemning venom. Then imagine them spoken with grace and compassion. Quiet your heart and listen for Jesus speaking your name, as he did Mary's.

18

Pregnant Father

My friend L'Anni was, back in the 1970s, one of the first women to be ordained in the Reformed Church of America. She was working as a hospital chaplain when she was pregnant with her first child.

Visiting patients room by room, L'Anni wore a clerical shirt most commonly recognized as being worn by Roman Catholic and Episcopalian priests: a black button-down cotton shirt with a white tab. When you're wandering the hallways of a hospital eight months pregnant and are five feet tall and almost as wide, I don't suppose it hurts to have something of a uniform to identify you as clergy.

Toward the end of her shift, L'Anni approached the bedside of an older Roman Catholic gentleman. Glancing up, without really registering the presence before him, the man quickly greeted her, "Hello, Father."

Isn't that a yummy little moment?

This accidentally progressive father-mother combo was understood, at some level, by St. Augustine. With reference to Psalm 27:10, where the psalmist exclaims, "My father and mother have

Checkes & Joff

abandoned me," Augustine understands something of the fullness inherent in God's parenting. Augustine writes, "The speaker has made himself a little child before God; he has chosen Him as his father, he has made Him his mother. He is a father because He has created him, because He calls him to His service, He directs him, He governs him: a mother in that He cherishes him, feeds him, suckles him, nurses him."[1]

God's Mothering and Fathering

To say that God is the one who mothers and fathers us opens up a wonderful wellspring of possibility to receive from God what it is we most need. It's a beautiful, heartwarming sentiment.

To attempt to flesh it out, though, is asking for trouble.

Christians who would tend toward a more conservative and traditional theological bent would be completely satisfied with God's fatherhood, finding no lack in it, and might be *wary* of making room for God's motherhood.

But Christians who view the faith more liberally, who might be very open to receiving God's care as both mother and father, may take issue with any attempt to assign gender-specific functions to "mother" and to "father."

You can see how it becomes a pickle pretty quickly.

> To say that God is the one who mothers and fathers us opens up a wonderful wellspring of possibility to receive from God what it is we most need.

For instance, Frank Lake maintains, "There are two vital needs of every child in these foundation years, which could be summed up as the face of the mother and the voice of the father; the smile of loving recognition and the word of guidance."[2]

While I'm of the mind that God longs to meet these very basic needs in this very primal way, Christians on the right may want to pull in the reins on the explicit "mothering" of God and those more on the left may want to put a kibosh on the particularity of what the mother gives to the child and what the father gives.

I mentioned it's messy, right?

Since you're bound to have opinions of your own, I suspect that, to your ear, *either* Lake's view of God as mother makes you a little uncomfortable *or* Lake's reliance on gender stereotypes sounds hopelessly outdated. Acknowledged. And I encourage you to remain flexible enough to stay with this business as long as you can. The fact is, Lake has identified two legitimate human needs: to be recognized and nurtured as well as to be spoken to and sent.

> The bottom line is this: God gives us what we most need.

The bottom line is this: God gives us what we most need. He provides us with what our mothers lacked and with what our fathers lacked.

To name God as *parent* is to be claimed by God as *child* and is, in a very particular way, to have access to the eternal resources of the face and voice that do not fail.

Being Nurtured by the Face of God

According to Lake and others, in the face of the mother the child develops personal identity. The gift the mother gives is recognition and unconditional acceptance. Her face affirms and nurtures. From the mother, the child learns her worth. Our hunger for a smile of welcome and loving recognition is met, or unmet, in the face of the mother.

Thousands of years ago, to put flesh on the holy face, God commissioned his priests, in the line of Aaron, to bless the people he loved by shining forth God's holy face (Num. 6:22–27).

Poetic in form, the original beauty of the Hebrew has been lost in translation. In each of three lines, the first clause in each line begins by identifying the LORD as the subject. The first line has three words, the second line five words, and the final line has seven words, expanding each idea a bit further.

The English translation reads,

> The LORD bless you and keep you;
> the LORD make his face to shine upon you, and be gracious
>   to you;
> the LORD lift up his countenance upon you, and give you
>   peace. (vv. 24–26)

I've listened to these words *hundreds* of times on CD as part of the lyrics to a Michael Card song that was the lullaby sung and played for my young children at bedtime.

The first line references God's "blessing" and "keeping." Hearers would have known that God's blessing included land, health, progeny, and God's own presence. God's keeping was to protect them from evil. The two in tandem are the beautiful faces that Frank Lake identifies as the mothering and fathering gifts of God: the face that nurtures and the face that protects.

The second line of the blessing amplifies God's graciousness, using the image of light to describe God's face shining upon the people.

The third goes a bit further to "the active movement of God to lift up his face and send blessing and grace specifically toward the people."[3] God's blessing culminates in the final word, *shalom*, which suggests the fullness of health, prosperity, and salvation.

In God choosing *this* blessing by which the priests would bless his people, he is painting a vision of the best possible reality for their wellbeing. The very *best* thing you could pronounce over a people is that they'd receive good things and be kept from bad things. They'd see God's face shining upon them, and God would even go to the trouble to *lift* his face toward them to bless them. All that is good—kids and grandkids, home, land, health, and God's very own face—is included in this blessing.

The very best, best, best thing you could say to a person was that God's benevolent face would be tipped toward him or her.

And the way God extended that blessing to the ones he loved wasn't through an ancient scroll or stone tablets. It was through the human faces of God's prophets and priests and parents, the agents God used, and still uses, to form and transform.

When human faces do this thing—shining the truth of God's gracious welcome through their actual faces—they represent the gracious welcome of God.

Baptism

Though my parents did not baptize me as an infant, my approach to the font was, though more conscious, no less rote than the rite applied to so many infants. At First Presbyterian Church of Glen Ellyn, Illinois, my friends and I, as ninth graders, had dutifully completed a year of confirmation class. In May we would go before the church to confirm our faith in Jesus. Most of my friends, those of churchy parents, had been baptized as infants. I was one of two confirmands who had not.

I announced my faith in Jesus and, as I knelt at the front of the sanctuary, three scoops of water were ladled onto my head. And with that, it was official: I belonged to God. And though I can't pretend to grasp the mystery, it was efficacious. The moment defined me in a particular way. Though it would, as years passed, be easy enough to dismiss—as the contrived result of religion, or peer pressure—it also carried with it meaning I could choose to embrace.

The moment of my baptism was, and is, to make a choice *for* welcome. For acceptability. For belovedness. It's to choose to identify myself as one who has been received, once and for all, irrevocably, never to be forsaken. In this way, according to Frank Lake, baptism is symbolic of the *mothering* of God. The gracious welcome of God's face becomes accessible to us, in a very visceral way, through baptism. Lake explains, "The once-for-all sacrament of baptism is the sign of God's *acceptance* of us. . . . This declares the existence of a pact of love and assured acceptance which is always God's work, not ours."[4]

In our baptism, sin and shame are washed away entirely. In Christ, they are no more. Each time I choose to grasp the reality of my utter acceptability to God, each time I cling to the story of my baptism, I embrace the story that is true. In it, I choose *for* the pact of love and assured acceptance God has established.

In baptism, the face of the mother shines, confirming, "This is my child, the beloved, with whom I am well pleased."

In baptism we receive God's smile of recognition and acceptance.

Being Addressed by the Guiding Voice

Just as we are *received*, accepted in the most fundamental way, by the mothering face of God, we are also called out into the world by the voice of the father. The voice of the father offers provision, guidance, and sending.

While the mother's face offers personal identity, in the voice of the father, the child develops social identity, discovering who she is in relation to others and in a world of meaningful activities. From the father, the child discovers her mission. Our hunger for a guiding and sending word is met in the voice of the father.

The fundamental story of the Old Testament is one of sending and provision. When God's people were stuck and enslaved, the voice of God called out to Moses from a burning bush. Through Moses himself, God called his people out of slavery and into freedom. Like the voice of the human father, God calls the child out from dependence upon the mother into the freedom to trust God for provision.

For the Israelites, the guiding voice that called them into freedom was also the One who provided for their needs. Each day God would rain down manna from heaven, and each day God's people would have enough. God was, for them, a good Provider and a guiding sender.

At the Table

Lately, I have felt far from God. I go through the religious motions, but I don't feel a sense of God's presence. I comfort myself in the fact that I heard the same was true of Mother Teresa. For years she prayed and served, prayed and loved, prayed and obeyed . . . when she did not *feel* God's palpable presence. *If being spiritually dry was good enough for that saint*, I tell myself, *it's good enough for me.*

That I go through the motions means, among other things, that I show up for church. I stand when I'm supposed to stand. I sing, most of the time, when invited to sing. I don't always have the stamina to make it through to the benediction, often rushing out early under the guise of some excuse or another.

A few weeks ago, sitting in the balcony with wiggly, scribbly, giggly children, I stood when the deacon wearing a red vest told me to stand and I dutifully followed the other people in my row toward the station where two elders were serving communion. Though I should have been thinking about how Jesus died so I could eat his broken body, I kept noticing the communion servers.

Each of these men had, at one time or another, been for me the very face of God in some of my darkest moments. In several cases, it was in just this way: serving me communion that fed my hungry soul. In other times, each one had spoken just the right word or offered a gracious hug. Seriously, with three communion stations happening in various spots in the sanctuary, it almost didn't make sense to have all that firepower up in the balcony where just a handful of us could receive from them. It would have made more sense to space these guys out across different weeks, rotating them through the different locations.

But there they were, *for* me.

By the time I'd reached the front of the line, I felt emotion welling up behind my eyes.

"Margot." Russell beamed, offering a plate of bread, "This is Christ's body, broken for you."

"Margot." Markus smiled gently, holding forth the holy cup, "This is the blood of Christ, shed for you."

At the makeshift, invisible table where two men of God stood in a crowded hallway, I was *addressed* by the voice of God. I was fed with bread and with spirit and with person. I was nourished and sent back into the world, strengthened.

At the table where Jesus fed his disciples with his own body, we are invited to be fed, sustained, and guided by God.

Frank Lake narrates the gracious gift God gives at the table:

> The *sustenance* of the life God gives to His adopted children is not something they have to work for or could merit. . . . Of course, we must change our habits of biting our nails, so to speak, and hold out our hands to His holy Food in the Sacrament.[5]

When we stick out our hands, God feeds. God provides. God leads. God sends.

Font and Table

At the font we are, irrevocably, received by God. At the table we are, dependably, fed by God.

The mothering face of God says at the font to those who long for unreserved welcome, "I am with you and I am for you."

The fathering face of God says at the table to those who hunger for provision and guidance, "I am with you and I am for you."

The face and voice of God are available to all who would turn toward him.

We're "mothered" by priests whose faces shine God's own countenance upon us. We're mothered as we receive God's welcome at baptism. We're mothered as God's face shines through those who reflect, for us, the truth of our identity and God's. We're mothered as we receive God's face through the living presence of Jesus.

We're "fathered" by God's goodness in calling our ancestors out of slavery and providing for them in the wilderness. We're fathered as we're fed by God in the Eucharist. We're fathered as God's voice speaks through those who reflect, for us, the truth about who we are and who God is. We're fathered as we receive God's Word through the person of Jesus. We're fathered as we're sent off to participate in God's mission in the world.

Frank Lake notes that Jesus had access to the mothering and fathering of God, in a very particular way, through the prayers of the psalms. In those prayers, he claims, God's face and voice were revealed. As they were used to form and sustain Jesus, so too they are available to us. Lake confirms, "The Holy Spirit will use these prayers for us, as He used them for the Son of God Himself, as a revelation of the Face of God and the Word of God, the mothering and the fathering of the eternal Source of Being."[6]

Thanks be to God.

At the font, God mothers you by accepting and receiving you exactly as you are. There God shines upon you, affirming you. At the table, God fathers you by feeding and sustaining you. There God's voice sends you into the world. Pause to consider which you most need today. Then meet God either at the font or at the table—remembering your baptism or reliving the Lord's Supper—and allow God to give you what it is you most need today.

We Receive God's Gracious Face

onvinced we're accepted by God as we are, and not as we should be, we're at last liberated to be who we really are. Confident that God's kind face shines upon us, living mask-free, we choose to live into the reality of our belovedness. In this, we also offer to others the wonderful possibility of doing the same.

19

Why I Love My Grandmother's Fabulous New Face

For me and my squirrely children, Sunday morning worship can feel like the very last place any of us want to be. Though I can't speak to their reasons, mine is no secret: it is *them*. That my husband and I expect them to be there at all absolutely infuriates them. Though they might have just been having the time of their lives downstairs at Sunday school, shoving donuts into their mouths *while* playing Ping-Pong, somewhere between the entrance to the sanctuary and filing into the pew I'm saving, each one shoots me a look that lets me know they blame me for . . . every bad thing that ever has or will happen to them in their lifetimes.

Church with them really is *that* unpleasant.

Though it's a complicated subsequent procedure to block out whatever is happening to my right—usually the loud tearing of paper of making confetti out of pew-pocket prayer cards or the vibration of Lego-marching across the shoulders of the person in front of them—I try my hardest to block them out while allowing worshipful things to enter my left eye and ear. As someone who gets easily overwhelmed by multiple stimuli, this is no small feat.

The service was close to being over when, glancing toward the back of the sanctuary, I noticed a young man, Kevin, walking down the aisle and heading for the pew behind me. Kevin is a new college student and was probably home for the weekend. For the last eleven years I'd seen him dutifully sitting in one of the front rows with his folks and younger sister. They are a great family. And I cannot say enough good things about Kevin's parents. They are just salt-of-the-earth people: warm, kind, smart, faithful. Though we don't spend a lot of time together, everything I know of them is good.

As Kevin stepped over a child to wiggle his way into the pew, I began wondering how it works with churchy kids after they go off to college. Are they mandated to attend worship when they're home on vacation? Do they go if they wake up in time? Are they exempt if they pretend to sleep? Do they still try to cause a pew-ruckus to let their parents know how displeased they are to be there? I do not know. I certainly don't know how it works at Kevin's house. But because I do hold Kevin's folks in such high regard, I made a mental note to ask them how I should do it in the future.

Specifically, because the service was almost over, I was curious how Kevin's family would react to the timing of his arrival. Would they be disgruntled because, for whatever young adult reasons, he was late? Would they be a little embarrassed that everyone had seen him clump in toward the end of the service? I didn't know.

I perked up my ears to eavesdrop.

Politely scootching past a few more people in the row, Kevin wedged in next to his mom. And though I didn't turn around, I paid close attention.

In a church-volume voice, somewhere between whisper and regular, Kevin's dad said, "Good to see you."

Gracious Voice and Face

"Good to see you" could have been spoken any variety of ways, right?

If Kevin's dad had been an emotionally stunted, passive aggressive man, "Good to see you" might have rung with an ugly edge of sarcasm.

But it didn't.

If Kevin's dad was seething mad, furious because he'd told Kevin to be there promptly at eleven, then "Good to see you" might have dripped with bitter vitriol.

But it didn't.

If Kevin had been due to arrive home from school the previous evening, and hadn't been reachable by phone, and his folks had been worried sick, and maybe even called the police, then "Good to see you" might have been full of both anxiety and relief.

But it wasn't.

No, in fact, the greeting Kevin received stopped me dead in my pew. Though it was just the four words—"good to see you"—the affect behind them overflowed with graciousness. In those four little words, it became entirely evident that Kevin's dad *delighted in his son*. Whether Kevin was late, or wearing crazy earrings, or hung over, or coming from sleeping at his girlfriend's was entirely irrelevant. What was entirely evident to my ear was that the mere fact of Kevin's presence caused his dad absolute *delight*.

Though I could not turn around to *see* Kevin's dad, I knew, in the deepest way, that his face *lit up* at Kevin's arrival. And though I understand that it's not technically possible to see with your ears, in that moment I actually did. It would be physically impossible to sound that genuinely pleased to see someone and not show it on your face: eyebrows rising, eyes widening slightly, mouth-ends tipping upward as the pitch of your voice rises a bit.

When the Aaronic blessing in Numbers 6 says, "The LORD make his face to shine upon you," it means that God's face shines like the face of Kevin's dad. A face shines, it lights up, as it communicates absolute graciousness to the one basking in its glow.

That Kevin's dad was absolutely delighted to see his son could be heard in his voice and seen on his face.

Faces That Mirror What Is True

I've begun to collect these mental thumbnail images of the face that is good.

Dr. Andrew P. Morrison offers several precious glimpses of human faces that do not shame. Specifically, as they gaze upon what actually may *be* unacceptable, like Kevin's late church arrival may have been, they accept nonetheless.

> When Bobby brings home a drawing from nursery school of a man shooting a robber, his mother is, internally, a bit disconcerted. Gathering her wits, she gushes, "That's really neat, Bobby! I like the color of the shooting coming out of the gun." She then suggests to Bobby that his father would like to see it after work. When this father is shown the picture, he is enthusiastic and asks Bobby to tell him the story of the picture.[1]

Without shame, these parents *receive* their son.

Morrison also describes the relationship between a young girl named Alice and her mother. "Alice was an assertive, headstrong little girl who was clear in her preferences and wishes and frequently pushed to get what she wanted," Morrison explains. Reading between the lines, I deduce that Alice is a pain in the patootee. He continues, "Alice's mother, herself a confident and assured person, valued her daughter's 'grit' and curiosity." He explains, "She always had a gleam in her eye for her daughter, even when Alice was at her most mischievous."[2]

Without a hint of shame, Alice is received exactly as she is.

I see this gracious reception in the eyes of some of the parents I know who are raising children with disabilities. A number of these, who are long past the point of wishing their children were other than they actually are, have become able to accept their children in a way I think might be unique to parents of children who have various lifelong challenges. Perhaps, at some point, the faces of these parents were scared or disappointed or angry or sad. But when they have reached a point of acceptance, many of these—in a way parents of more typical kids might not ever achieve, those who are always secretly hoping their kids will achieve a wee little bit more—practice a radical acceptance of their children. Accepting, these are faces truly able to delight in their kids, exactly as they are.

These human faces bear the reality of God's steadfast, gracious presence to the precious ones God loves.

Glimpses of the True Face

In the 2003–5 TV drama *Joan of Arcadia*, fifteen-year-old Joan encounters God in the form of various characters woven throughout each week's episode of the show. Though the award-winning show was on air for just two seasons, its credits list a fabulous array of God-figures. All played by different actors, the colorful list includes but is not limited to: Dog Walker God, Goth Kid God, Garbage Man God, Balloon Sculptor God, Mime God, Bad Stand-Up Comedian God, East Indian Sunglasses Salesman God, and Gay Male Secretary God. To name a few. Fantastic, right?

Jessamyn Neuhaus's contribution to an anthology title *Doing More with Life*, describes the nature of *Joan of Arcadia*'s deity. This one, she explains, is an "unknowable but visible God, who sees and is seen and is among us always, in all kinds of forms, participating in our everyday life but not interfering with humanity's free will, and who nonetheless calls us into service."[3] So Joan's God isn't so unlike the trinitarian one in whom Christians believe.

I spent the few episodes I watched comparing the writers' representations of "God" to the ones I'd encountered in Scripture. So if a pimply teenager was outraged about injustice, I'd nod and muse, *That sounds like the agent of justice I've met in the Old Testament.* If a grandmother walking past a crying, hurt child in the park scooped the toddler up in her arms, I'd think, *Yup, that looks like the God who gathers chicks under divine wings.* If a carpenter walking through a seedy alley paused to share a bag of chips with the despised, I'd figure, *Yeah, that does seem like Jesus.*

When we think we recognize God's face on human bodies, we compare it to what we know to be true of the One revealed in Scripture, and if it looks like the God-face we can see on the person of Jesus, we know it's a match.

Fortuitous Reflections

Once I purposed to notice reflections of the divine countenance, I began to catch glimpses of it in human faces. Sort of like that tortured Joan of Arcadia. And, without trying, I began to recognize its absence as well.

Though my husband and I weren't raised during the Great Depression, we can both, at times, behave as if there's a significant shortage of resources and our rigid rationing of supplies is sort of a life or death situation. I suspect this has to do with us both being youngest children who at one time lived in the shadow of voraciously eating older brothers. For instance, our children have picked up on the fact that we both act a little weird about orange juice. A small glass of juice, first thing in the morning, is acceptable, but after 8:00 a.m., we do not want our children drinking more juice. The outrage of afterschool juice, in both of our minds, borders on criminal. There's one gallon in the fridge, and if it's going to sustain all the juice-drinkers in the house, it needs to be rationed.

I mention this because the deeply ingrained anxiety about the orange juice stands in stark contrast both to our shared wish to be generous with others and to the face of the man who fed five thousand with a few loaves. The ugly truth is never more evident than when our neighbor, eleven-year-old Dattu, comes over. Like so many eleven-year-old boys, he's often hungry. So he wants to know what types of food we have in stock. Dattu's favorite thing from our freezer is frozen chicken patties. So it's not like he's demanding fresh caviar. He's just craving a little protein.

These patties have been a real opportunity for growth for my husband and I. Our *instinct* is to say, "No. No patties." What's absurd is we don't even know *why*. We want the boy to eat. We have patties. We have the resources to buy more patties. We're just very damaged people.

> **When we think we recognize God's face on human bodies, we compare it to what we know to be true of the One revealed in Scripture, and if it looks like the God-face we can see on the person of Jesus, we know it's a match.**

The absurdity of the patty situation is that as small and stingy and controlling as Peter and I are about orange juice and chicken patties, Dattu's family is oppositely, and abundantly, generous. When I've been at their house, starving for a snack, and have asked to pilfer something small from their awesome snack pantry, they're almost *confused* by my asking. Of *course* I can have something from their pantry! What's theirs is mine.

That "of-course-you-can-you-crazy-nutball" expression is, for me, a glimpse of the face of a God who gives out of gracious abundance. It matches the face of Jesus's father.

Accepting a Serial Killer

I also get a glimpse of God's gracious reception in the face of my friend Gair, with whom I try to walk each week.

I could be wrong about this, but I'm pretty sure I could start one of these walks around the local golf course by confessing to a string of serial killings, and with empathy and compassion she'd embrace me and check in on how I'd been feeling since the murders. Wanting to make sure I was okay.

She's like that. Not in a sick way, either. But in the nothing-you-could-tell-me-could-change-my-affection-for-you kind of way. And while I'm sure she'd contact the Durham police department on her cell after hugging me goodbye and before her car had left the lot where we meet, her feathers aren't easily ruffled.

And in those unrufflable feathers, I recognize the mother-hen wing of God that nestles me in good and tight.

Airport Stalker

I'll tell you where else I see God's face: at the airport. Specifically, after I've hoisted my bags off the conveyor belt. I'll linger around like a creepy stalker if I've noticed a mom and her kids anxiously waiting for Dad to come down the escalator. If it's late at night, the kids might be wearing their pajamas. They'll hop around, nervously, waiting for him to show up. No one is bickering with each other because everyone is so happy they're about to be reunited.

Though I'm not a big one for public displays of emotion—specifically *mine*—these scenes really do me in. If it's a boy waiting on his dad, I might be able to hold back tears. If it's a girl, there's no chance I won't be bawling the moment that dad shows up. I try to talk myself down by telling myself he probably just went to New York on business for the day. But if the dad descending the escalator toward the baggage area is wearing a military uniform, and I believe in my mind that he's been gone for nine months, there's no telling how loud I'll wail.

Usually in these situations, the mother will try to hang back as the kids maul their father. She won't demand a lot of attention. The kids will run into daddy's arms and get swung around, or cling to his waist or leg, as he fights his way toward his bride. With children smashed between them, they create a family hug-sandwich.

I tell you, I'm a sucker for these moments. In them I see the face and voice and body of God. And if you asked me if I was seeing God in the itchy toddlers who are on pins and needles to see Daddy, or if God was the reliable dad who returns to his family, or if God was the mom who makes it all possible by working and feeding the babies and giving the baths, I would just say, "Yes." For in that messy tangle of people at the bottom of the escalator are those who embody the very descriptions Jesus used to describe what his Father is like. I see the woman who's totally psyched to have found her lost coin and the father who welcomes a prodigal son. I recognize the gracious nurturer-provider of the psalms and also the face of the One who returned from the dead never to leave again.

Does that pile of people look like the God pictured in the Bible? Yes.

A Gracious Voice

A couple of friends of ours, who are rather high-profile and are pretty well-connected in the town in which we lived, were going through a rough patch. And by "rough patch," I mean that their lives had completely fallen apart at the seams.

One of the hindrances of being well-connected in these situations, I'm told, is that it's hard to find a counselor or therapist that doesn't already know you, your parents, and the name of your dog. And although these therapeutic professionals are trained in the art of confidentiality, Hank and Jennifer (the first fake names I thought of) wanted to find someone with whom they did not already have a relationship.

As someone who's come unglued on more than one occasion, I completely understood.

Jennifer did what so many of us do in these sorts of emergencies. She googled for help. Specifically, she searched for Christian counselors in our town. Faced with all 197,000 results, she clicked on the first few and browsed bios. When she found one that was a match, she made her phone call.

Sadly, after Jennifer explained to therapist Ron a bit about their situation, she learned that he no longer had an office in our town. And though he was in a nearby town, he wouldn't be able to see them for a few days. Graciously, he offered to recommend someone else.

By that time, though, there was no way Jennifer was going to talk to anyone besides Ron. In the brief exchange, when all he'd actually said with words was that he wasn't able to meet with them immediately, she'd heard something in Ron's voice that convinced her that *this* was the helper for them.

From the particular way in which Ron had said "I'm not available"—belying his compassion, kindness, graciousness, and generosity—Jennifer had become convinced that this was the counselor who would be able to help them.

Really, that's what she got from "No."

If it's possible for a voice to offer hope, and later for the matching face to facilitate redemption, Ron's most certainly had. Now, a year and a half later, Jennifer can't say enough good things about Ron.

She explains, "We needed a kind voice. He saved our lives."

That a "No" can be filled with generosity and grace sounds exactly like the kind voice of God.

An Accepting Face

The gracious face of God is wildly evident in my grandmother's face. Though she lives with dementia, and honestly in part *because* she lives with dementia, her face receives others as we actually are. Though when she was in her "right mind" she was judgmental about nose rings and tattoos, disturbed by rock music, fearful of cat diseases, and disgusted by words like "poop" and "fart," her countenance is different now. She accepts my nose ring and my cousin's tattoos. She allows rock music on the car radio, even enjoying it. The cats she once considered so disease-ridden as to be life-threatening she now enjoys. And bathroom words like "poop" and "fart" now give her the giggles.

As you might imagine, she is a *delight* to be around. Her family loves her. The folks who care for her love her. And, really, who *wouldn't*? Each one of us longs for the face that receives us exactly as we are and—not unlike the receiving face of an infant—my grandmother's face has become, in the most comprehensive way, that glorious countenance.

Hers is a decidedly salvific face. To be with her *heals* my deep places. Because she embodies the deepest reality of God's unbridled acceptance, I leave feeling as though I really am acceptable. Exactly as I am.

Who are the faces in your life that have shined upon you with unconditional love and acceptance? Whose voice has rung with compassion and truth and kindness? How do they communicate, to your heart, what God's presence is like? Put yourself into the "airport scene"—getting off an airplane to be greeted by someone who's thrilled to see you—and allow yourself to be received, entirely, by God.

20

"Yu Mine. I Yuhs."

I was really poor when we were growing up," explains Michelle. "For instance we would share one cup of noodles as a family of five. I had a baby brother during that time and we didn't have milk for him. We fed him water from rice. It wasn't really a good life, when we grew up."[1]

Entrenched in despair, raised in the Philippines, Michelle lived with sixteen other family members in a small shanty. She was surrounded by violence, gambling, and drug abuse. Around her Michelle saw friends sold into prostitution.

To the extent that children naturally believe that they deserve whatever it is they get, poverty lied to Michelle about her value and worth. Her relatives reinforced the lie, telling her both that she was ugly like her father, a drug user, and that she would never become anything when she grew up but a thief and a drug addict. Michelle explains, "I felt so hopeless that I really didn't matter and that I was not important."

Poverty, and the voices of those around her who confirmed it, told Michelle she wasn't worth much and wouldn't become much.

The only Christian Michelle knew was her aunt. Some members of a local church that partnered with Compassion International told her aunt, "If you want to change your niece's life, enroll her in the project." At the project, the children's physical, social, emotional, and spiritual needs were met by members of the church. Michelle explains, "Going to the Compassion project was like a haven for us. It was a place where we would be fed. We would be treated well and people would really love us."

When Michelle started the program, at age six, she didn't understand that the program through her local church was made possible because of sponsors abroad.

She explains, "I think I was about seven years old when I got my first letter from my sponsor. Their names were Tom and Esther Brasile from the United States. I really love them. They wrote me letters and I still have all of them."[2] With tears in her eyes, Michelle recounts, "My sponsor told me: Michelle you are beautiful, you are precious to us and we love you."[3] In conjunction with the steadfast, faithful care Michelle received from Compassion staff through her local church, the words spoken by Tom and Esther, and the faces behind them, transformed Michelle's life.

Hearing this much of Michelle's story made me itchy to find out what sort of image she connected to God's face. Knowing it was a long shot that she'd have a memory of how she perceived God during the first six years of her life, I asked her. She told me, "When I was growing up, the picture of God in my mind was that of a very rich man who is so strict and hard to please."

Dispelling that early image was no small feat. Through the years, Michelle wrestled with that picture and its impact on the way she saw herself and the world. She explains, "The picture has changed through the years of walking with the Lord and learning more of what the gospel really means."

Despite the early human faces that lied about her worth, the face Michelle has given to God has changed. Isn't that amazing? God can use experiences of human faithfulness to meet the deep needs of our hearts and to show us his face even more clearly.

If I had to guess, I'd suspect that Michelle's picture of God now looks a little more like Tom and Esther.

Faces That Redeem

Alice Miller was a therapist whose life work focused on adults who'd experienced abuse or neglect in childhood. Miller's work was not limited to physical violence or sexual abuse, which, she asserted, could be more easily recognized and discussed. Rather, her deep concern was mental abuse, the destructive ways in which parents interact with their children.

These are the ones Michelle heard say, "You'll never amount to much."

It's the mother who badgers a daughter ceaselessly about her weight.

It's the father in the football bleachers, who's been shamed himself, who screams shaming words at his awkward benchwarmer or gifted quarterback son.

It's the raging mother, herself the victim of rage, whose glaring countenance communicates as loudly as words her perception of her child's worth.

It's the insecure stepfather who bullies a stepson.

It's the mother who, while he's doing the bullying, looks the other way.

> God can use experiences of human faithfulness to meet the deep needs of our hearts and to show us his face even more clearly.

In her book *The Drama of the Gifted Child*, Miller describes how victims can hide the conscious knowledge of the pain of these experiences even from themselves until some sort of crisis or trauma in later life exposes it.[4] Like me, they armor up. So though the individual might consciously remember the treatment he or she received, the pain attached to it may remain buried.

Miller was convinced that the singular solution to childhood pain—the type festering silently beneath the stubborn masks we wear—was not to plaster over it or skirt around it, but to head straight through it.

The Significance of One

Research demonstrates that individuals who do experience childhood pain will often repeat the cycle that they experienced as children. For example, studies have shown that each adult who is physically violent with a child has, herself or himself, been the victim of violence. Each parent who shames a child on the ice rink or grassy field or hardwood court has similarly suffered shaming words. Cycles of violence and shame are repeated in families and societies generation after generation.

But here's where it gets interesting: though each incident of violence toward children can be traced back to the known or unknown experience of the abuser, the converse is not necessarily true. Though every abuser has *been* mistreated, not every child who endures abuse will grow up to perpetuate the violence themselves. This gripped the imagination of Alice Miller. In fact, it drove her to discover what was particular about the experience of those who grew to thrive that released them—and their children!—from the destructive bind.

Miller discovered that every one of these individuals who'd been able to stop the destructive pattern shared *one thing* in common: each one had had access to what Miller called a "helping witness." The helping witness is an adult whose face reflects for the child the truth of their worth. This helping witness could be a coach, a teacher, a neighbor, an aunt—anyone who would reflect the reality of a child's value.

It's the aunt who tells the child of an addict, "You are so very precious, baby."

It's the scout leader, recognizing telltale bruising, who confirms, "This shouldn't be happening to you."

It's the accepting parent of a friend who rejoices, "You are delightful. I'm so glad to know you."

It's the husband of a mentally ill wife who tells his daughter, "Your needs matter to me."

It's the mother who's just left an abusive husband who asks her son, "What is this like for you, sweetie? I wonder how you might be feeling now."

It's the grandfather, with a twinkle in his eye, who assures a grandchild, "I'm so glad you're mine."

It's the neighbor who assures a neglected child, "I think you're a very special boy."

It's Esther and Tom, and it's Michelle, who say, "You are precious to me and I love you."

Even if the adult is not able to change the child's difficult circumstances, claimed Alice Miller, he communicates to the child that she deserves more, she is *worth* more, than her circumstances suggest. The countenance of the helping witness confirms, "You're *worth* protecting. You're *worth* loving." Children who have access to a face like this are the ones who grow to survive and to thrive. These are the ones who are eventually able to parent their own children differently, because they've had access to a single reliable witness.

I find this thrilling.

Absence of the Needed Face

Miller also dealt with those individuals who simply did *not* have access to a gracious face who confirmed their worth. In Miller's work with jailed offenders, she recognized grown-ups who had, as children, been without that reliable face affirming their value. What she discovered, though, was that when those adult prisoners had an "enlightened witness," one who would walk with them as they dared to face the pain they'd endured in childhood, they experienced authentic emotional transformation. With conviction, these gracious faces, confirming that the man or woman was inherently worth protecting and nurturing, accompanied them in the difficult journey of recognizing and feeling the pain of their lives.

The face that aids in this transformation may be the friend journeying with the woman who's just been left by her husband. She's the voice who says, "I don't know if you've heard this today, but you are an amazing woman and you are precious to me."

The face may be the one that accompanies the adult who's searched for and found a birthmother who doesn't want to know him. He's the voice who says, "I'm so, so sorry she's not able to welcome you. You are worth receiving."

The face might be the one that is traveling alongside a friend whose child is dying. It's the voice who says, "This must be excruciating. Your child doesn't deserve this and you don't deserve it."

The faces willing to look at our pain, both recognizing and honoring it, are the faces that reflect the gracious acceptance of God to us. They confirm we are *worth* loving.

Dawn

For years, when Dawn would hear people in church call God "Father," and when they'd pray on Father's Day for all the fathers who had shown what God is like, Dawn simply felt void. Lost. Disconnected.

Her father, a veteran suffering from both post-traumatic stress disorder and bipolar disorder, had been an alcoholic since Dawn's youth. During the years she lived at home with her parents, he was abusive to Dawn and to her mother.

It was not until Dawn married—remarkably, a man who was nothing like her dad—that she had even an inkling of what all those well-meaning church people meant. It happened as she watched her husband *father* their children.

When Dawn shared this much with me, I *had* to know more.

"Tell me how that is! Tell me about him!" I demanded.

There is a part of me that is still strangely warmed when I see fantastic dads in action. And in whatever measure the Spirit allows, I try to soak up a little bit for myself. Even if I'm just a creepy listening-stalker, like I was with Dawn.

As she described her *husband*, I suspected I would be able to use that description to infer something both about her early experience of her father and also something of what she once believed about God.

"My husband isn't perfect, but he's consistent," Dawn bragged. "He is always available, always supportive, always even and fair."

What I thought I could infer about Dawn's father was confirmed when she explained, "My father could turn on a dime: sweet and fun one minute, throwing you across the room the next. I actually think it would have been better if he was mean all the time, because then I would have known to always steer clear."

My first reaction to Dawn's description was that, had it been me, I would have just hedged my bets and steered clear all the time. But, of course, girl-Dawn was *wired* to receive care and connection from her father. Hungry for it, she no doubt tried to scavenge what she could.

Dawn continued to describe her dreamy husband. "He is a soft place to land. Very rarely is he fazed at all by emotional outbursts from me or the kids. He calmly talks through the situation and helps set you back on track. I guess he reminds me of Jesus out on the Sea of Galilee as the storm rages about. He calmly and patiently talks the wind and waves down."

As the words passed her lips, Dawn could hear how she's come dangerously close to deifying her husband. She backtracked. "Of course he's not *God*. Of course he's fallible. Of course he gets offtrack at times. But his nature, his essence, is very much like what I think the writers of the Bible were referring to when they called the Lord *Abba*. Until I saw a clear view of a father unmarred by war, mental illness, and addiction, I never could refer to God as Abba Father. There was such a disconnect."

Today the disconnect is being bridged by a gracious *physical* presence. "There are still some unhealed wounds," Dawn admitted. "But now, as God is redeeming the loss in my life by giving my kids, and essentially me, a true father to love and enjoy, I get it. I have even caught myself praying, 'Heavenly Father' and 'Thank you, Father.'"

Grace was appropriated, by Dawn, through a human face.

For most of us, reading the words in a holy book, void of tangible, physical incarnation, is not changing us. Encounters with people, encounters with the Holy Spirit—that's what changes us.

A Reparative Face

Brennan Manning, born "Richard" Manning, lived for years bound by the childhood shame he was dealt by his mother and even by the clergy. In young adulthood, however, he experienced one of these transforming human faces. In his memoir *All Is Grace*, Manning describes an experience he had in a college speech class. After delivering his speech, and receiving a positive response from the class, his professor asked to see him briefly.

"Richard," the teacher said, "you've been given a great gift. Use it well."

Manning explains:

> That was the first time anyone had said anything about my ability to speak. . . . I'm hesitant to say my professor's words changed everything, but they did change something, something about how I saw myself. Sometimes one sentence can stand up against years of hearing "He won't amount to much."[5]

The face of that professor spoke the truth to Manning's parched heart.

Though Alice Miller would not have recognized these gracious faces as being agents of *God's* truth, Henri Nouwen understood them in exactly this way. In his collection of personal affirmations, the words he heard God speaking to his soul during his darkest days, Nouwen shares, "The love that came to you in particular, concrete human friendships and that awakened your dormant desire to be completely and unconditionally loved was real and authentic. . . . The task is not to die to life-giving relationships but to realize that the love you received in them is part of a greater love."[6]

The source of the greater love is the Face that is true.

In raising my son Abhi, who'd come to be with us through adoption, I long for that sustaining *greater* love to be made manifest through our family.

As he was learning to speak, I taught Abhi to repeat after me the chalky Valentine-heart-candy slogans, "I'm yours . . . you're mine."

When we'd cuddle in bed, I'd have him repeat after me.

"I'm yours . . . now you say it . . ." I instructed him.

"I yuhs," he dutifully parroted.

"You're mine," I said. "Now you say, 'You're mine.'"

I'm entirely convinced that this re-forming business is what God is about in human lives.

"Yu mine," he replied.

The pair of couplets quickly became our own private ritual.

"I'm yours."

"I yuhs."

"You're mine."

"Yu mine."

During his earliest years we would whisper them to one another at bedtime, and while snapping together carseat buckles, and when saying goodbye at YMCA childcare. It became the wonderful secret, between just us, that made us both smile.

To one another's hearts, we spoke the words that are deeply true. I pray that they impacted him and I feel certain that those words—*from the eyes of a child who accepted me exactly as I was, and the lips of a mother who understood loss*—re-formed me.

An Unfortunate Message Bearer

I'm entirely convinced that this re-forming business is what God is about in human lives.

Specifically, it's what God's prophet Hosea was speaking to God's people during the eighth century BC. At the heart of the message God had given to Hosea was that God's people had been unfaithful, forsaking faithfulness to Yahweh by accepting other gods. The

Israelites, believing these other Canaanite gods made the land fertile, had divided their allegiance to the one true God, Yahweh.

The Lord's call to Hosea, in the midst of this crisis, was heart wrenching, "Go, take for yourself a wife of whoredom and have children of whoredom, for the land commits great whoredom by forsaking the LORD" (Hosea 1:2). Hosea, doing as he was told, took for a wife a prostitute, a woman named Gomer, who bore him three children.

God instructed Hosea to name the first, a son, Jezreel, meaning "*God sows.*" The context suggests God is not planning on sowing daisies, but instead punishment.

God told Hosea to name his second child, a daughter, Lo-ruhamah, meaning "*not pitied.*"

God told Hosea to name his third child, a son, Lo-ammi, meaning "*not my people.*"

In what feels like a particularly cruel assignment, God promised, through Hosea's witness, "In the place where it was said to them, 'You are not my people,' it shall be said to them, 'Children of the living God'" (v. 10). God, who longed to draw an unfaithful people back to himself, used Hosea's family as the thumbnail sketch of what was and what was to be.

While I desperately want this to be a symbolic story, an allegory of God's steadfast faithfulness, prophets embodying God's Word—literally, with symbolic actions—is prevalent throughout the writings of the prophets.

So, God bless you, Hosea.

A Family Renewed

Hosea's prophecy begins by detailing charges against Hosea's wife, against God's Israel, which is patterned after the legal process, from indictment to punishment. Accused of unfaithfulness, her punishment is made explicit (2:1–13).

Despite her wickedness, and with no prerequisite of faithfulness henceforth, God announces his gracious intention toward this one who is unfaithful. With the most tender language, God describes drawing his lover to himself, speaking tenderly toward her, and eliciting her loving response. The fulfillment of this covenant of love is made explicit in two sections. The first is that of a husband addressing his wife, pledging steadfast love and faithfulness. The second section expresses the restoration of Hosea and Gomer's children. In this poetic reversal, God undoes the curse of each name that had been given.

Of Jezreel, *God sows*, God announces, "I will sow him for myself in the land" (v. 23).

Of Lo-ruhamah, *not pitied*, God declares, "I will have pity on Lo-ruhamah" (v. 23).

And of Lo-ammi, *not my people*—the child of Hosea whose hurt resonates with the deep wound of my own heart—God also reverses the curse by saying to him, to Israel, to God's own, "You are my people" (v. 23). Here, though, in contrast to the passive subjects Jezreel and Lo-ruhamah, we are privileged to hear the response of Lo-ammi.

God's prophecy, through Hosea, announces: "I will say to Lo-ammi, 'You are my people'; and he shall say, 'You are my God'" (v. 23).

The true words of God are meant to re-form our broken human hearts.

I imagine Hosea curled up with his children at bedtime:

"You're mine."

"Yu mine."

The witness of the Scriptures has convinced me that communicating the abiding truth of his gracious love to human hearts is God's big business.

Woven throughout the message of God's prophets is the assurance that, despite all we have committed and incurred, God is faithful to the covenant he has established. Again and again God promises, of people who have been forsaken, "They will call on my name, and I will answer them. I will say, 'They are my people'; and they will say, 'The LORD is our God'" (Zech. 13:9). In matters of theocracies, and the private lives of cursed prophets, and even in the hearts of little boys and little girls, grown boys and grown girls—based on no merit of our own—the God who sees the scars borne by our cursed hearts comes to us in tenderness to call us his own.

The face and voice of God, through the Word that is true, re-form us into who we really are as God's beloved.

"We're God's."

"God's ours."

Inextricably.

Alice Miller called the adult face who sees and reflects the reality of another's difficult early experience an "enlightened witness." Is there someone available to you who can listen to your story, affirm it, and reflect God's compassion for you? You can also address the Holy Spirit in this way. By speaking or praying or journaling, allow God to see every bit of your past. Then, notice what expression you see on the face of God toward you. What words of affirmation does God speak to your heart?

21

Lookin' for Love

As I searched for the face that was true—in Scripture, in Jesus, in human faces—a naughty little voice in my head would taunt, *God heals others, but not you. God's gracious face is revealed to others, but not to you. You are alone, abandoned, and forsaken.* And though I wish it were not the case, as you purpose to choose the face that is True, you can expect to meet similar resistance.

Resistance will come in any number of forms. It may be that a friend's Facebook post gushes about how grateful he is for fourteen years of marriage to an *amazing* spouse. Though you're happy enough for him, that little voice whispers, *Sure, it's easy for* him *to experience God's love. Because he has it in a reliable human person.*

Or perhaps you have another friend who is very connected to the face and voice of God. She actually *hears* God speaking sweet nothings in her ear. A shaming voice hisses, *You simply aren't spiritual enough to recognize God's gracious face. Maybe if you just prayed the right way. . . .* Or the deceiver will suggest, *You're just too broken. Why bother?*

Henri Nouwen also recognized this naughty voice. Emphasizing the personal responsibility we have to choose, day after day, *for* life, he underscores, "The root choice is to trust at all times that God is with you and will give you what you most need." It's to agree with what is true, to choose *for* God's voice, and to reject the lies about who we are. In my experience, these voices have a belligerent quality. They're loud, brash, pushy, and intrusive. Their noise drowns out the steady, calm, quieter voice that is true.

Nouwen continues, "Still, you know that these are not God's voice. God says to you, 'I love you, I am with you.' . . . This is the voice to listen to. And that listening requires a real choice, not just once in a while but every moment of every day and night."[1]

In the moments I most need to hear this voice, I'm tired and worn and weary and it's much easier to hear and heed the lying voice that insists there is no hope. This voice resonates with the pain reverberating on my emotional circuitry. But Nouwen counsels, speaking to his own heart, "As you keep choosing God, your emotions will gradually give up their rebellion and be converted to the truth in you."[2]

Recognizing God's Face in Scripture

To aid in our search for the face of God, we have been given the Scriptures, where God's countenance is most clearly revealed. The singular place where we're able to distinguish the ungodly faces we've held in our hearts from the One that is real, where we're able to glimpse the almighty, everlasting God, is in the face of Jesus, who, Paul insists, is "the image of the invisible God" (Col. 1:15).

Because we're too often tempted to give the invisible God a face other than the gracious face of Jesus, we're obliged to compare the likenesses we hold in our hearts and minds to the living person of Jesus who's revealed in the Gospels.

Clearly, this is easier said than done. If it were *that* easy, anyone who'd cracked open the good book would be wooed by the face for which they most longed. We bring all sorts of baggage to our reading, masking God and disguising Jesus. As we invite the Spirit to show us the face that is true, though, we're given eyes and ears to see God's gracious face and hear his gracious voice.

I'm convinced that on every single page of the Scriptures God's face shines and God whispers to human hearts, "I am the One who is with you and for you." Should you randomly open the Bible and drop your finger on some horrific tragedy—the slaughter of the innocents, the rape of Dinah, or babies having their heads bashed against rocks—close your eyes, quiet your heart, and listen. Despite human horror, and perhaps most particularly in the midst of it, God's voice continues to speak, "I am the One who is with you and for you." His may sometimes be a tearstained face, but it is reliably present throughout the Scriptures.

Two particular places that God's face can be glimpsed most clearly are in the Psalms and in the Gospels. As we eavesdrop there, as others relate to God in the Psalms and as Jesus engages with people in the Gospels, we see what God is like. As we open our eyes to receive a face that is gracious, the Spirit shows us the face, and lets us hear the voice, of the One who is good.

Encountering God's Presence in the Holy

Like the wise Dr. Loder invited folks to do, we also experience God's face when we return to the authentic experiences we have had of the *holy*. My friend Melissa was kind enough to share her amazing story with me.

Melissa fidgeted and wiggled as she sat on a chair in my living room. Though willing to share with me, she still seemed a little nervous. After doing drugs for four years, at just nineteen years old, she'd been drug free for nine months. Over those four years she drank, she was sexually promiscuous and, by her own admission, she was hurting.

About a year earlier, Melissa had had a really bad acid trip. In it, she was filled with rage. She explained that, though she wasn't a person of faith, she had an awareness that Satan was controlling her at that moment. "I felt like I was really in hell," she said. Into that odd scene, Melissa saw the person of Jesus and felt peace. She explained, "Jesus was basically saying to Satan, 'No.' He couldn't have me because I was his child. It was really weird." And though she continued to do drugs after that experience, they lost their intense effect.

Unable to shake the impact of the encounter, Melissa visited the neighborhood church her grandmother attended to speak to the pastor. There she was received, seen, and heard. She was also prayed for. As she continued to sort out her life, Melissa began to consider turning her life over to Christ.

Melissa explained, "One night voices were talking to me about everything that hurt from the past. I was really scared and I was sick of it. So I prayed. It was like a whisper-cry-pray. And I went to sleep right away. About two hours later I woke up. I was shaking when I woke up. And you could hear like a roar, like an angry roar, like a frustrated roar, and then there was peace in me. And everything that was hurting and making me angry left and then I had God-peace in me. I think the roar was what was affecting me at that time. Because it wasn't me roaring."

In both her bad acid trip, and also the sleep-waking roar, Melissa had encountered the holy. She'd encountered the palpable presence of God.

From that point on, when the naughty voices returned, Melissa would have a choice. As she became a little more sophisticated, it would have been easy enough for Melissa to say, "Wow, those drugs really messed me up," or "I really had a scary dream one time." But instead, Melissa continued to choose *for* her experience of the holy. That God had entered her broken world, making himself known, was the pivotal moment of Melissa's life. To choose *for* it was to ground herself in reality. For years to come, to choose for God's true word, "She belongs to me," would ground Melissa in the truth of God's great love for her.

Have you encountered the living presence of God? Has there been a moment, or moments, in your faith journey when you knew

God's nearness? Continue to choose *for* those moments. Allow yourself to be formed by them.

Seeing the Face of Jesus

We *always* encounter the face of God in the person of Jesus. That's where we see it clearly. And the apostle Paul's insistence that Jesus is "the image of the invisible God" (Col. 1:15) makes it sound really simple to see God's face. We look at Jesus and there it is.

In one respect, it really is that simple.

But it's important to recognize that there's another face that competes for attention. Even when we've conceded to a warm, gracious Jesus, we're often still tempted to keep the image of a foreboding Father in our back pockets for bad measure. For so many complicated reasons we have difficulty trusting that there's no difference in character and personality between the Father and the Son.

For this reason, a fellow named Rev. Martin Davis insists on the importance of bringing believers face-to-face with God in Jesus Christ. Davis says that Jesus "defines God for us and does so in a way that calls into question all alien presuppositions about God."[3]

> For so many complicated reasons we have difficulty trusting that there's no difference in character and personality between the Father and the Son.

Isn't that just the most beautiful sentence using the word *alien* you've ever heard? When we come face-to-face with God in Jesus—the very one who defines God for us—all our "alien presuppositions" about God are called into question. So rather than slapping whatever mask we've given to God onto Jesus—whether Angry-Old-Testament Deity or Abusive-Like-My-Father Deity or some other equally disturbing façade—we instead allow the human face of Jesus that can be seen and heard in the Gospels to define and inform what we know of God.

In the face of Jesus the alien presupposition that God is a weak, impotent deity bound by the wiles of Satan is destroyed.

In the face of Jesus the alien presupposition that God is seething with rage at humanity for doing things we can't avoid doing is dissipated.

In the face of Jesus the alien presupposition that God's face seeks to punish us is dissolved.

In the face of Jesus the alien presupposition that the face of God mirrors the formative faces in our lives who were unable to offer us gracious welcome is dashed.

The face of Jesus, the gracious one, is meant to replace the inadequate faces through which we have presupposed what God is like.

This is really good news, people.

As you encounter Jesus in Scripture and in prayer, invite the Spirit to open your eyes to the face that is good.

The Particularity of *God for Us* on the Cross

There is one particular moment in my journey—like Melissa's acid trip and roaring God, though not nearly as awesome—when I encountered the holy One. I'd been reading Alice Miller, and I understood that one of the most important resources for kids who'd been through the wringer was to have access to a reliable adult face who reflected, for them, their worth. At the end of my rope, I demanded God show me the face of someone who had been *for* me when I most needed it. Raising my fist to the heavens, I begged, "Where was that face?"

Wafting down from heaven, like a floating feather—maybe one that had gotten loose from the dove at Jesus's baptism, floating Forrest Gump–style for centuries—were two words that simply landed in my heart: *I am.*

As I am not one who is prone to hear God's voice speaking directly to me, I resisted.

I just thought those two little words because I've read them in the Bible, I reasoned. *That's the dumb name that God gave when*

Moses asked him for ID. And then it was the one used by Jesus time and time again. I am the light. I am the bread. I am the way. I am the gate. Oy! Those words just bubbled up from my subconscious. Since God does not talk to me.

As I continued to protest, two additional words landed in my heart. This time with more of a *thunk*: *I am for you.*

God wanted me to know not just a surface expression of my belovedness, but a reminder that I am loved *to death*.

I am for you? Had I seen those on a license plate? A greeting card? Surely they were being regurgitated, like a bad meal, from some deep place in my gut. And as I continued to resist, to deny that I was being addressed by the One who is real, I saw an image of Jesus Christ on the cross.

Though it wasn't an image I'd chosen, not one toward which I would typically turn, in that moment it brought such clarity of meaning to my experience. As I raged at God, demanding to know who he'd provided to be *for* me, God wanted me to know not just a surface expression of my belovedness, but a reminder that I am loved *to death*.

It was as if grace rushed into my deep places, filling up the dry, barren cracks. Though I'd always believed, deep down, that I was unacceptable, I suddenly became aware of this fundamental experience of Jesus dying on the cross for *me*. And because he had been *for* me—in ways my caregivers had been unable to be—I came to know myself as acceptable. As worthy of being loved. Because I'd been accepted in such a fundamental way, I suddenly came to know, in my bones, that I was worth accepting. The sinister, cyclical logic of shame with which I'd lived for so long—that because I'd been left I wasn't worth loving—had been turned on its head by the deep experiential knowledge of God's great love for me in Christ's sacrifice *for me*.

As you search for the gracious face of God, there is a particularity to Jesus's death and resurrection that informs God's posture toward you.

God Made Visible through Books

Whether you stand directly in front of her, a little off to the left, or far back to the right, it appears that the knowing gaze of Mona Lisa is riveted on *you*. And though thousands of visitors to Paris's Louvre museum will eyeball her day after day, year after year, there is that certain . . . je ne sais quoi . . . *impression* that she's looking back at you.

There are books that have a similar appeal. Though the particularities of the author's story may be dramatically different from the reader's, by the final page the reader feels as though she has been *seen*, because the author has, in a way, articulated what is true of her own story.

As has no doubt become apparent, one of the most beautiful road maps in my journey has been a thin volume from Henri Nouwen called *The Inner Voice of Love*. My brother gave it to me. In the wake of his own personal "dark night of the soul," a season of anguish and despair as he questioned his identity, Nouwen journaled a series of powerful personal imperatives. After each session with a trusted guide, pen in hand, he would seize the command that had emerged during the session. Though he did not intend for these personal reflections to be published, when he shared them with friends they urged him to release them for publication. And while he resisted due to their personal nature, he did eventually relent, just months before his death.

If you're a person who's tipped your face toward a rejecting face, you really need to get your hands on this little masterpiece. Underlined, highlighted, dog-eared, and scribbled-in, my own copy was like cool water during my own wilderness wanderings. You don't want to guzzle it down, though. Its efficacy is in being savored, as if allowing an ice cube to melt on your tongue. A short half-page entry, or even a single sentence, can be a feast for a day or week.

As I finished the volume, I mused to myself, *Though I don't know the details of Nouwen's despair, it really seems as if he must have endured just exactly what I've endured.* I also happen to know for a fact that a loved one of mine, whose story is diametrically different from my own, closed the back cover and thought to herself, *Though I don't know the exact details of Nouwen's despair, I'm pretty certain that he must have endured exactly what I've endured.* Therein lies the gift. Having stripped the text of those tender bits particular to his own devastating season of loneliness, Nouwen created a book that has this dynamic quality of seeming to recognize and address, in very particular ways, the heart of each reader.

Like the mysterious gaze of the Mona Lisa, it will look you right in the eye.

What book has God used that has allowed you to see God's face anew or hear God's voice in fresh ways? For some, it may be a memoir or novel that describes another's journey toward the face that is good. For many, *The Shack* was a story like this. For others, it could be a theological journal. For others, it could even be a book on parenting that describes the kind of face and voice children need.

If you hadn't considered this way of seeing God's face before, keep your eyes open!

God's Face Reflected through Others

We also encounter God's face through the faces of others. Particularly the faces of those who are members of Christ's body.

As a child, Sandy's family didn't practice any religion. Left to her own musings, she had always thought that if there *was* a God, he would be like her dad: unobservant, not caring, always angry. When she did come to know God, through Christ, in college, it took Sandy several years to get to a place where she could pray to God as "Father." When asked about how she views God today, Sandy will sincerely say that she views God as a patient, totally involved, and loving Father.

So how did that happen?

When I asked what expression she sees on God's face, Sandy chimed, "Delight!" Since she'd decidedly *not* gleaned that from her earthly father, she explains, "I don't think I ever experienced delight until I became a Christian and saw it in the face of others who have loved me ferociously."

Sandy really sees that whole thing as a chicken and egg situation. Namely, she can't quantify which came first. She mused, "Either the more I experienced it in others, the more I believed that the Lord felt that way about me too . . . or . . . the Lord was gracious enough to give it to me through others in very tangible ways."

I had a special someone in my life who did for me what those gracious faces did for Sandy.

Arriving too early for the drama department's annual production at the end of my second semester of college, I decided to kill the extra minutes in the school library. I was browsing through old yearbooks when a stranger approached and addressed me.

"Has anyone ever told you that you have the aura of Harrison Ford?"

What sounded like a cheesy barroom pickup line was the last thing I would have ever expected to hear at the library on my small college campus.

Looking up, I came face-to-face with a woman in her late thirties. She introduced herself as Sharon. A writer, Sharon had graduated from Westmont two decades earlier. I was actually browsing through a yearbook that included her picture when we met. This signaled to Sharon that we were meant to know each other.

That evening we ended up attending the performance together. Though I never was entirely clear about the particular defining features of Harrison Ford's aura, and never thought to ask, my meeting with Sharon turned out to be the beginning of a wonderful friendship. During the years I lived in Santa Barbara, Sharon would invite me to her beautiful ocean-view home for meals and conversation and old movies. Leading me through her house and out to the back porch for the first time, she announced, "My body likes to exercise facing green." And with a quick glance toward the landscaped garden behind the porch, she bent over and touched her toes.

I had never even thought to ask my body what it liked to face while exercising.

When I was away from Santa Barbara one summer, Sharon wrote to me, beginning her letter, "Dear Margot, You *must* be a texture person because I felt compelled to write to you on my best linen paper." Though at the time I questioned whether this intuitive gift was really one God gave, I would come to discover of myself, years later, that I really am a texture person.

Sharon thought that the historical moment when I entered the world was significant. She wanted me to know that the summer I was born hippies were running around Woodstock and the Kennedys were playing football on their lawn in Hyannis, where I'd been conceived.

Despite her granola packaging, I found Sharon to be a woman of deep and abiding faith in Jesus Christ. My experience of her was that she really *saw* me. And, apparently, my aura as well. To the degree that she could perceive what I could not yet, I felt like she knew me better than I knew myself. The fact that she had initially spotted me, or at least had sensed my aura, made me feel as though I'd been chosen. It felt like a very special gift to have been noticed, accepted, and pursued. *Really* wonderful.

My experience with Sharon was that I was recognized and received exactly as I was. Through her face, I was given God's own eyes. In it, I saw *delight*.

God's Presence as You Reflect It to Others

I suspect that as others reflected God's face for Sandy, and as Sharon reflected it for me, they came to know God's graciousness even more deeply in their own hearts. It's like learning to read. If you scan the words quietly with your eyes, you read them once. If you speak them aloud with your lips, you read them twice. As the sound enters your ears, you're reading them a third time. When you read aloud, when you practice offering God's steadfast face to others, you receive it again yourself.

I've noticed this most palpably in relation to my children.

A late-night glimpse of my slumbering four- or five-year-old daughter peacefully sprawled on new pink paisley sheets would not have caused *every* mom to choke up. And yet, pausing in the hallway to notice the security she enjoyed—both physical and emotional—touched a deep hurt in my own heart. Having given myself to pricey therapy just hours earlier, I was keenly aware that the stinging *absence* of stability like this in my own formative years had, over time, formed me, complicated my marriage, and impacted my parenting.

> **When you practice offering God's steadfast face to others, you receive it again yourself.**

At her age I'd had no idea that I was worth loving. And yet when this little girl came into my life, I *instinctively* knew it. *Of course every child is worth loving and nurturing and protecting!* I knew it to be undeniably true for my children and I hoped that it was true for me. What had been stirring inside me for the first five years of my daughter's life was an invitation not only to provide a safe home for her, and for my sons, but to allow the loving presence of God to dwell *with me*, daily. Now, watching my girl dream unburdened girlie-dreams, keenly aware of her undeniable lovability, there was no doubt in my mind that every single child is inherently *worth* loving.

My growing edge during those early years, of course, was to allow "every single child" to include even me. As love flowed through me to her, a bit of the commonsense "Of course every kid is worthy" began to rub off on me. George S. Merriam claims, "At the times when you cannot see God, there is still open to you this sacred possibility, to show God; for it is the love and kindness of human hearts through which the divine really comes home to men, whether they name it or not."[4] Prepared or not, I was the channel through which God's love for my sweet babies would flow.

Graciously, a bit of that love rubbed off on me in the process.

To be a channel of God's love isn't the sole domain of parents. God's love flows through each one of us to friends and parents and dogs and neighbors and coworkers. And as it does, God's good intention is that a bit of love is left behind.

Holy Rendezvous

If you're like many Christians, you're willing to believe that when you were first claimed by Jesus you were touched by a perfect love. Chances are good that you're also willing to stand on the firm promise that when you take your final breath, you will be received into God's gracious arms with a love that does not fail.

But what about *now*? Are you willing to claim and live into God's steadfast love for you, as you are, *right now*?

Pause to imagine Jesus standing before you with outstretched arms. With open palms, Jesus holds each of your heartfelt bookend moments in his lifted hands. In one hand is the memory of knowing his love to be true in your past, and in the other hand is the hope that you will know it once again.

Notice his face. How Jesus's kind eyes meet yours without a hint of condemnation. Recognizing all that you have been, are, and will be, his face is full of gracious love for you. In this face, you are welcomed as you have been by no other human face.

> But what about *now*? Are you willing to claim and live into God's steadfast love for you, as you are, *right now*?

As you receive and are received by him, you may also recognize a familiar voice hissing into your ear, *You're not good enough. You're not worthy of love.* This is not God's voice. The lying whisper is silenced as you choose *for* the voice that is true. This is the voice that says, "I am *with* you. I am *for* you."

The voice that is true says, "Don't be afraid, I've redeemed you. I've called your name. You're mine" (Isa. 43:1–2 Message). You are "chosen and marked by my love, delight of my life" (Matt. 3:17 Message). "I've never quit loving you and never will. Expect love, love, and more love!" (Jer. 31:3 Message).

As you glance up at Jesus, you see his outstretched arms. What you notice, today, is not a memory or a hope. You become aware of Jesus's gracious, unfailing love *in this moment*. With you. For you. Exactly as you are.

Gently, Jesus moves toward you to embrace you.

You are seen. You are known. You are heard. And you are loved.

Whatever your size, his arms wrap around you and, as they clasp behind you, the circuit is complete. You are held by a love that knows you intimately. His unbridled acceptance feels scandalous. Extravagant.

Because it is.

You are seen. You are known. You are heard. And you are loved. In this moment, and in all others, he is altogether with you and for you.

Suddenly wondering how you'd missed it until now, you purpose to continue to choose *for* the undeniable truth of your belovedness.

And that changes *everything*.

Open yourself to God's Spirit, removing all limits and preconceptions about how God can and will meet you. Allow the Spirit to put to death any "alien presuppositions" you may still hold about who God is. Know that God's grace is not simply for others. It is for you. Quiet your heart and listen for God's voice speaking to your heart: **I am the One who is with you and for you**. If you have difficulty centering in on this reality, locate yourself at the cross of Christ and receive, anew, his sacrifice of love for you.

Acknowledgments

Thank you to all those who were willing to share their stories—those who are recognizable and those who are not—especially the ones you'd rather not own. You have given a precious gift to me and to many others.

Much gratitude to those who first introduced me to the guiding voices that have helped *me* to recognize the face, and hear the voice, that is gracious: Scott Starbuck for Henri Nouwen, Jon Wilcox for Lewis Smedes, Leanne Payne for Frank Lake, and Bart Tarman for Brennan Manning. You, and they, have been transformational.

Thank you to Greg and Becky Johnson for their enduring TLC and their steadfast belief in my writing.

Thank you to Zoe, Rollie, and Abhi. Because each one of you is so stinkin' *easy* to love—to find altogether precious and worthy and amazing—I am able to taste a sliver of what the Father's relentless affection for me is like. Thank you for the unwitting gift.

Thanks, above all, to the One whose love does not, and cannot, fail.

Notes

Introduction

1. Lewis Smedes, *Shame and Grace* (New York: HarperOne, 1993), 80.
2. Ibid.
3. Ibid., 46.

Chapter 1 The Face That Smiles

1. Holly Riley, *Allowing: A Portrait of Forgiving and Letting Life Love You* (Bloomington, IN: iUniverse.com, 2010), 11.
2. Ibid., 11.
3. Ibid.
4. Ibid., 12.

Chapter 2 Forty-Two Bucks

1. Allan and Barbara Pease, *The Definitive Book of Body Language* (New York: Bantam Books, 2004), 167.
2. Ibid.
3. Ibid., 169.
4. Ibid.
5. James Alison, "Love Your Enemy: Within a Divided Self," lecture, St. Martin-in-the-Fields Church, London, England, October 30, 2007.
6. Ibid.
7. Frank Lake, *Clinical Theology* (London: Darton, Longman & Todd, 1966), 627.

Chapter 3 The Making of a Snack Closet Bandit

1. Henri Nouwen, *The Inner Voice of Love* (New York: Doubleday, 1998), 101.
2. Brene Brown, *The Gifts of Imperfection* (Center City, MN: Hazelden, 2010), Kindle edition.

3. Ibid., 53.
4. Lake, *Clinical Theology*, 181.
5. Ibid., 166.
6. Brown, *Gifts of Imperfection*.

Chapter 4 Sophisticated Eye Transplants

1. Brene Brown, *I Thought It Was Just Me: Women Reclaiming Power and Courage in a Culture of Shame* (New York: Gotham Books, 2007), xxv.
2. Garrison Keillor, *Lake Wobegon Days* (New York: Penguin, 1990), 323.

Chapter 5 Pay No Attention to the Tiny Shoulder Devil

1. *The Kid*, directed by John Turteltaub (Disney Studios, 2000), DVD.

Chapter 6 Too Much Lipstick

1. *A Knight's Tale*, directed by Brian Helgeland (Columbia Pictures, 2001), DVD.
2. J. S. Rusby and F. Tasker, "Childhood temporary separation: long-term effects of the British evacuation of children during World War 2 on older adults' attachment styles," *Attachment and Human Development* 10(2), 207–221, http://www.ncbi.nlm.nih.gov/pubmed/18773319.
3. James S. M. Rusby, "Effect of childhood age in foster care on the incidence of divorce in adulthood," *Journal of Family Psychology* 24(1), February 2010, 101–4, http://psycnet.apa.org/journals/fam/24/1/101/.
4. Smedes, *Shame and Grace*, 53.

Chapter 7 Spidey's Getting the Love

1. Lake, *Clinical Theology*, 5.
2. Ibid., 745.

Chapter 8 Because We're Not Land Snails

1. Kim Carollo, "Makeup Makes Women Seem More Competent, Study Says," *Good Morning America*, October 4, 2011, http://abcnews.go.com/Health/cosmetics-make-women-likable-competent-trustworthy-attractive-study/story?id=14659706.
2. Emma Gray, "For Women, Going Makeup Free Is More Stressful Than First Date, Job Interview," *Huffington Post*, March 20, 2012, http://www.huffingtonpost.com/2012/03/20/women-makeup-free-stressful-first-date-job-interview_n_1366541.html.
3. Edmond Rostand, *Cyrano DeBergerac*, trans. Mary F. Guillemard and Gladys Thomas (Project Gutenberg, 2009), http://www.gutenberg.org/files/1254/1254-h/1254-h.htm.

Chapter 9 Supermom Made Her Kid Cry

1. Smedes, *Shame and Grace*, 110.

Chapter 10 Be Who You *Are*

1. Nouwen, *Inner Voice of Love*, 13.
2. Anne Lamott, *Grace (Eventually)* (New York: Penguin Group, 2007), 80.
3. Ibid., 79.

Chapter 11 An Infinite Number of Elrods

1. Baylor Institute for Studies of Religion, "American Piety in the 21st Century: New Insights to the Depth and Complexity of Religion in the US," September 2006 (www.baylor.edu/content/services/document.php/33304.pdf), 4.
2. Ibid., 26.
3. Ibid.
4. Ibid., 27.
5. Ibid.
6. Ibid.
7. Ibid.
8. Ibid., 28.
9. Brennan Manning and John Blase, *All Is Grace* (Colorado Springs: David C. Cook, 2011), Kindle edition.
10. Ibid.
11. Ibid.

Chapter 12 My Mom's Face on Jesus's Body

1. Lake, *Clinical Theology*, 183.
2. James Loder, *The Transforming Moment* (Colorado Springs: Helmers & Howard, 1989), 163.
3. Lake, *Clinical Theology*, 181.
4. Loder, *Transforming Moment*, 169.

Chapter 13 Gravy Boat God

1. Chris Willman, "Charlton Heston: The EW Interview," *Entertainment Weekly*, April 8, 2008, http://www.ew.com/ew/article/0,,20189905,00.html.
2. Andrew Newberg, MD, and Mark Robert Waldman, *How God Changes Your Brain: Breakthrough Findings from a Leading Neuroscientist* (New York: Random House, 2009), 87.
3. Ibid., 88.
4. Ibid., 89.
5. Ibid., 88.
6. William P. Young, *The Shack* (Newbury Park, CA: Windblown Media, 2007), 73.
7. Ibid., 82–83.
8. Ibid., 83.

Chapter 14 Longing to Be Delivered by a Redemptive Face

1. Dr. Eben Alexander, "Heaven Is Real: A Doctor's Experience with the Afterlife," *Newsweek*, October 8, 2012, http://www.thedailybeast.com/

newsweek/2012/10/07/proof-of-heaven-a-doctor-s-experience-with-the-afterlife.
html.

2. Ibid.

3. Ibid.

4. Ibid.

Chapter 16 Jennifer, Boy, Boy, and Boy

1. Jerry Parr with Carolyn Parr, *In the Secret Service* (Wheaton, IL: Tyndale, forthcoming).

Chapter 17 The Face of Infinite Compassion

1. Mary Neal, interview by Matt Lauer, *The Today Show*, July 19, 2012, http://www.today.com/id/48242202/ns/today-books/t/i-was-home-former-skeptic-shares-glimpse-heaven/#.UFN6oBjx87A.

2. Ibid.

Chapter 18 Pregnant Father

1. Augustine, *Volume 1 of St. Augustine on the Psalms*, ed. and trans. by Felicitas Corrigan and Scholastica Hebgin (Westminster, MD: Newman Press, 1960), 277.

2. Lake, *Clinical Theology*, 179.

3. Dennis T. Olson, *Harper's Bible Commentary* (San Francisco: Harper & Row, 1988), 187.

4. Lake, *Clinical Theology*, 206.

5. Ibid., 207.

6. Ibid., 186–87.

Chapter 19 Why I Love My Grandmother's Fabulous New Face

1. Andrew P. Morrison, *The Culture of Shame* (Northvale, NJ: Jason Aronson, Inc., 1998), 72.

2. Ibid., 75.

3. Jessamyn Neuhaus, "*Joan of Arcadia* and Fulfilling Your True Nature," in Michael R. Miller, *Doing More with Life* (Baylor, TX: Baylor University Press, 2007), 33.

Chapter 20 "Yu Mine. I Yuhs."

1. Kees Boer, "Michelle Tolentino—From Poverty to True Riches," *Positive Entertainment*, http://www.positive-entertainment.com/interviews/michelletolentino/.

2. Ibid.

3. "One Act," YouTube video, 3:50, posted by CompassionIntl on March 17, 2010, http://www.youtube.com/watch?v=4lW25nhiEaY.

4. Alice Miller, *The Drama of the Gifted Child* (New York: Perennial, 1997).

5. Manning, *All Is Grace*.

6. Nouwen, *Inner Voice of Love*, 48.

Chapter 21 Lookin' for Love

1. Nouwen, *Inner Voice of Love*, 113–14.

2. Ibid.

3. Martin Davis, "Torrance: Evangelical Significance of the Homoousion," *God for Us!*, July 4, 2010, http://martinmdavis.blogspot.com/2010_07_01_archive.html.

4. George Spring Merriam, *The Way of Life* (Boston: George H. Ellis, 1882), 86.

Margot Starbuck believes that God's face is much more gracious than many of us have even begun to imagine. She is the author of five books and speaks to audiences around the country about God's unflagging goodness. Margot is the author of *Permission Granted*, a regular contributor to *Today's Christian Woman*, and an editorial advisor for *Gifted for Leadership*. She lives in Durham, North Carolina, and enjoys connecting with folks at Facebook.com/Margot or at www.MargotStarbuck.com.

Also Available from
MARGOT STARBUCK

• • • • •

"This is a love story. Margot dares you, provokes you, woos you to imagine the limitless power of grace. On every page you hear the whisper of God's love, and you are invited to become that whisper to the world."

—Shane Claiborne, activist, author, lover, www.thesimpleway.org

Keep the Conversation Going!

Connect with Margot at
MargotStarbuck.com for more resources.

Margot would love to be with your group!

Invite her to your church or next event.